SWITZERLAND
SKI GUIDE

By Alistair Scott
and the Staff of Berlitz Guides

Series Editor: Christina Jackson
Assistant Editor: Amanda Hopkins
Editorial Assistants: Felicitas Krause and Alice Taucher
Design: Dominique Michellod
Layout and Vignettes: Max Thommen
Photography: cover and p. 161 Herbert Steiner, Werbedienst Bahnen der Jungfrau-Region; cover skier and pp. 70, 71 Disentis Tourist Office; pp. 2–3, 81 Bergbahnen Flims; pp. 11, 13, 17, 19, 43, 50, 56, 60, 61, 67, 77, 80, 99, 105, 109, 139, 140 Jürg Donatsch; pp. 114, 147, 150, 165, 166 Claude Huber; pp. 12, 119, 121 Mürren Tourist Office; pp. 14, 36, 37, 38, Arosa Tourist Office; pp. 15, 73 Engelberg Tourist Office; p. 24 Adelboden Tourist Office; p. 27 Andermatt Tourist Office; pp. 47, 116–117 Morgins Tourist Office; p. 55 Crans-Montana Tourist Office; p. 83 Grächen Tourist Office; p. 87 Grindelwald Tourist Office; p. 88 Hans Rausser; Grindelwald Tourist Office; pp. 92, 129 Gstaad Tourist Office; p. 95 J.-P. Guillermin, Haute-Nendaz Tourist Office; pp. 102–103 Lenk Tourist Office; p. 108 Lenzerheide Tourist Office; pp. 125, 126 Pontresina Tourist Office, p. 132–133 Saas-Fee Tourist Office; pp. 144–145 Verbier Tourist Office; p. 155 Villars Tourist Office; p. 157 courtesy of Burton Snowboards.

Acknowledgments

We wish to thank all the local tourist offices in the resorts, as well as the Union Valaisanne du Tourisme, for providing information, maps and photos, and ADAC Verlag GmbH, for allowing us access to the films of their piste maps. We are also grateful to the Swiss National Tourist Office in London, Swissair, the Swiss Federal Railways and the Ski Club of Great Britain for assistance.

Copyright © 1989 by Berlitz Guides, a division of Macmillan S.A., 61, avenue d'Ouchy, 1000 Lausanne 6, Switzerland. All rights reserved. No part of this book may be reproduced or transmitted in any form or by any means, electronic or mechanical, including photocopying, recording or by any information storage and retrieval system without permission in writing from the publisher. Berlitz Trademark Reg. U.S. Patent Office and other countries—Marca Registrada. Printed in Switzerland.
Library of Congress Catalog Card No. 88-72146

Cover photo. Kleine Scheidegg, Grindelwald; pp. 2–3 Flims.

CONTENTS

Switzerland and its Skiing		9
How the Resorts Have Been Assessed		18
The Resorts at a Glance (Comparative Chart)		20–21
The Resorts	Adelboden	22
	Andermatt	26
	Anzère	30
	Arosa	33
	Champèry	39
	Champoussin	46
	Château d'Œx	49
	Crans-Montana	52
	Davos	57
	Les Diablerets	63
	Disentis	68
	Engelberg	72
	Flims/Laax	76
	Grächen	82
	Grindelwald	85
	Gstaad	89
	Haute-Nendaz	93
	Klosters	96
	Lenk	100
	Lenzerheide-Valbella	104
	Leysin	110
	Morgins	115
	Mürren	118

Pontresina	122
Rougemont	127
Saas-Fee	130
St. Mortiz	135
Verbier	141
Veysonnaz	148
Villars	151
Wengen	156
Zermatt	162
Berlitz Ski-Info (Practical Information)	169
Some Useful Expressions (French)	192
Some Useful Expressions (German)	196
Index	200

Maps

East Switzerland 7; West Switzerland 8; Adelboden 23; Andermatt 28–29; Anzère 31; Arosa 34–35; Champéry 40–41; Portes du Soleil 44–45; Crans-Montana 52; Davos 58–59; Les Diablerets 64–65; Disentis 68; Engelberg 74–75; Flims/Laax 78–79; Gstaad Superski Region 90–91; Klosters 97; Lenk 101; Lenzerheide-Valbella 106–107; Leysin 112–113; Pontresina 123; Saas-Fee 131; St. Moritz 136–137; 4 Vallées 142–143; Villars 152–153; Jungfrau Region 158–159; Zermatt 163.

Although we make every effort to ensure the accuracy of all the information in this book, changes occur incessantly. We cannot therefore take responsibility for facts, addresses and circumstances in general that are constantly subject to alteration.

All ratings of resorts in this guide were made without bias, partiality or prejudice and reflect the author's own subjective opinion. The information on the facts and figures pages was supplied by the resorts themselves. Prices shown are the most up to date available from the resort at the time of going to press. They should, however, only be taken as an indication of what to expect.

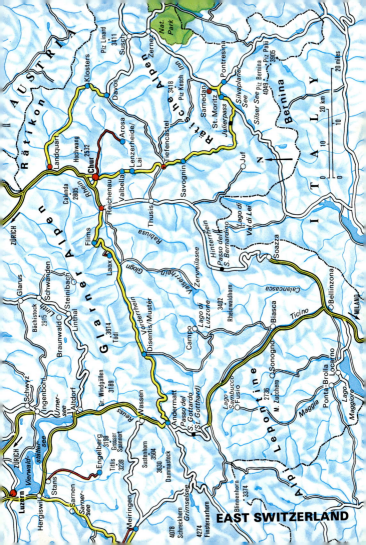

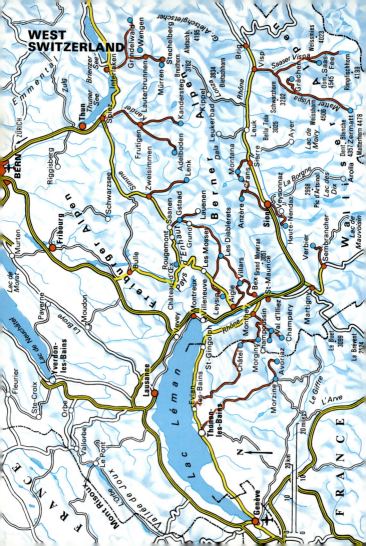

SWITZERLAND AND ITS SKIING

The British rightly claim to have invented the sport of downhill skiing, but they are proud of having done so in Switzerland. But even before the invention of the sport, the Swiss were already exploiting the tourist potential of their mountains in summer. Switzerland is the oldest skiing nation and that sense of tradition cannot fail to strike the visiting skier today.

Above all, it is the word "service" that makes skiing in Switzerland so special. As a nation the Swiss long ago recognized the importance of the tourist industry to their national economy. They are firmly resolved to give visitors to their country the best possible service during their stay.

Almost invariably this service is reflected in the price you pay. Switzerland is not cheap for foreigners but, as the Swiss never tire of pointing out, this is because of the weakness of the visitor's currency as opposed to the strength of the Swiss franc. (Switzerland's minimal inflation rate means that many hotel and restaurant prices remain the same for years at a time.) But although visitors to Switzerland may complain about prices being higher than in other Alpine countries, they will seldom have cause to complain about value for money or quality of service.

The Swiss are undoubtedly the world's best hoteliers and, although many of them now ply their trade abroad, there are still plenty of them left at home. Whether you choose a five-star or a one-star hotel for your Swiss holiday, you can be sure that standards of cleanliness and service will be the best in that category. Very many Swiss hotels in ski resorts are still run as family businesses, not as part of multi-national hotel chains, so the manager and/or chef may well also be the owner.

Switzerland is undoubtedly the most efficient country in the world, and it is a matter of national pride that any service that is advertised should be provided, regardless of freak snowstorms or any other obstacles. In other words the trains run on time and the ski lifts work so long as it is safe for them to do so. Reliable

SWITZERLAND AND ITS SKIING

public transport and efficient, safe lift systems are obviously a great attraction to the skiing holiday-maker.

In fact the Swiss public transport system is the envy of the world. Both the country's major international airports, Zurich and Geneva, have mainline railway stations incorporated. This means that you can load your baggage onto your trolley in the Baggage Reclaim hall and wheel it all the way to station platform. (The trolleys are even designed to ride with you on the escalators.) Even better, those travelling onward to their destination resort by train can register their luggage through independently—particularly useful if your journey involves changing trains. (On homebound journeys, passengers travelling by rail and scheduled flights can register their luggage through all the way from their resort to their destination airport.)

Many Swiss resorts are served by mountain railways which connect with ordinary trains at mainline stations. (Travelling from Geneva to Zermatt, for instance, you can take a through train from Geneva airport to Visp, from where you change onto a narrow-gauge train of the Brig-Visp-Zermatt railway which will take you all the way to Zermatt.) But even those resorts not served by railways are regularly served by reliable yellow PTT post buses.

Travel by road is also fairly easy in Switzerland. Access roads to all ski resorts are kept open throughout the winter except in very severe weather conditions. Nevertheless, it is always advisable to carry chains—better still have a four-wheel-drive vehicle—in order to negotiate the steep hairpin bends that lead up to so many resorts, as well as the roads in the resorts themselves, which often have snow on them for weeks at a time during the winter.

Switzerland's *autoroute (autobahn)* system, available to all vehicles displaying a specially purchased windscreen sticker, is impressive. Particularly useful is the *autoroute* running from Geneva airport, close to the French border, all the way along the north side of Lake Geneva and then along the Rhône valley to important valley towns like Aigle, Martigny and Sierre, from where a good main road runs on to Visp and Brig. The *autoroute* from Zurich to Chur is also of particular use to skiers.

But Switzerland is also an ideal destination for those skiers who want to spend their holidays away from vehicle exhaust fumes. It boasts some of the world's most charismatic car-free ski resorts,

Rustic chalet in Mürren affords a stupendous view.

including Zermatt, Saas-Fee, Wengen and Mürren. (However horses and silent battery-powered vans create hazards of a different kind!)

As far as ski-lift systems are concerned, there is no doubt that Switzerland has the most sophisticated and safest uphill transport in the world. Well-travelled skiers cannot fail to have noticed that many of the lifts which they have used in other countries have in fact been wholly or partly constructed by Swiss engineering companies. The Swiss have had funicular railways for decades.

There are still some old-fashioned rack-and-pinion railways in operation in places like Zermatt and Wengen. These are slow by today's standards, but also remarkably reliable and comfortable. On the other hand, Switzerland can also claim some of the world's most modern ski lifts, including two express underground funiculars: the Sunegga Express in Zermatt and the Metro Alpin in Saas-Fee.

Switzerland also has some of the world's most sophisticated cable-car systems, including that serving the Klein Matterhorn. The top station here is actually built into the mountain and, at a height of 3820 m., offers access to the highest skiing in Europe both winter and summer. In Verbier the 150-man "Le Jumbo" cable car from La Chaux to Les Gentianes provides easy access to the Mont-Fort glacier area throughout the year.

Switzerland has masses of télécabine and chair-lift systems, but it also still has plenty of old-fashioned T-bars. It must be said that these T-bar drag lifts often pose great problems for skiers who are not used to them—particularly people who normally ski in France where these contraptions are very rare.

But what of the skiing itself? The fact is that Switzerland has so many resorts offering such a range of skiing that there is quite literally something to please all types of skier. Indeed, many of the larger resorts have such a variety of skiing that experts, intermediates, beginners and even cross-country skiers can all be satisfied simultaneously. At the same time, there are resorts that cater particularly well for beginners and others that are suited to good intermediates and experts. Resorts like Verbier, Zermatt, Davos, Klosters, Crans-Montana and Wengen all have world-class skiing both on and off the piste. (Obviously it does not make sense for groups of complete beginners to pay the highest prices to go to the biggest resorts—they will simply be paying for lifts, pistes and other facilities that they will not be able to use.)

SWITZERLAND AND ITS SKIING

Switzerland also has a highly respected ski school—though as in any school some teachers are better than others—and unquestionably some of the best skiing mountain guides in the world. It is highly advisable that anyone wishing to explore the delights of Switzerland's off-piste skiing should do so in the company of one of these guides.

Unlike neighbouring France, Switzerland still permits the ultimate off-piste thrill: heli-skiing. This is of course expensive, but for those expert skiers who can afford it the lure is irresistible. Here again the presence of a qualified guide is essential.

Although non-skiers should generally be advised against taking skiing holidays, in the event that they do find themselves accompanying skiing friends, Swiss resorts can usually offer a good range of walks and other non-ski activities. Indeed from the majority of Swiss ski resorts it is possible to take day trips to

Après-ski possibilities range from ice-skating to sharing a fondue in a cosy mountain restaurant.

nearby towns and find places of interest. Lakeside towns like Montreux and Lausanne on Lake Geneva, and Interlaken, between the Thunersee and the Brienzersee, are particularly popular places for excursions.

Just because Switzerland is an efficient country does not mean that it lacks character. The problem is that it is a country that to some extent has a split personality. With its borders adjoining Europe's other three main skiing countries, Switzerland has borrowed and learned from all of them. Naturally skiers who consider themselves francophiles will probably be happiest in the French-speaking resorts, while those who are attracted to the

SWITZERLAND AND ITS SKIING

German or Austrian character or way of life will prefer the German-speaking parts. Yet every Swiss ski resort, no matter how close to the border it may be, remains defiantly and proudly Swiss. No other nation in Europe is as keen on displaying its national flag as Switzerland. On the mountainsides this flag is generally an indication of a mountain restaurant.

In fact, Switzerland has some of the best mountain restaurants to be found anywhere—consider La Marmite in St. Moritz or Enzo's Hitta in Zermatt—and the cuisine is usually truly international, borrowing from France, Germany and Italy, yet often also boasting uniquely Swiss dishes like potato *rösti*, raclette and the internationally known fondue. The Swiss also have their own local wines, though you will find these quite pricey in mountain restaurants.

Down in the village, most Swiss resorts offer a wide range of eating places, from pizzerias right up to gourmet restaurants. Although the meals you eat may not always be very exciting, you are very unlikely to be served a bad meal.

When it comes to après-ski activities, the usual rule for Switzerland applies: it may not be cheap, but it is good value. The Swiss do not insist on making their guests have fun in the evenings; they allow you to participate as much or as little as you like. In general the après-ski scene in Switzerland is sophisticated: there is not much yodelling and oompah bands are scarce. Nightspots such as the King's Club in St. Moritz, the Greengo in Gstaad, the Farm Club in Verbier and the Post in Zermatt are some of the smartest in Europe and are often mentioned in gossip columns.

The Swiss provide a warm welcome for visitors of all nationalities, but in many resorts there is always a particular affection reserved for the British. The two nations go back a long way together as far as Alpine activities are concerned, and a mutual respect born a hundred years ago or more still endures today.

In the end the only way to appreciate properly the very special attractions of Switzerland as a skiing country is to go there with an open mind and discover the country and meet the people. It would be surprising if the service and hospitality you received and the skiing you enjoyed on such a visit did not make you resolve to make a return to the slopes of Switzerland very soon.

HOW THE RESORTS HAVE BEEN ASSESSED

Different skiers have different requirements, and their choice of resort is influenced by many factors. In addition to the resort descriptions and facts and figures sheets, we have assessed each resort in nine categories, rating each aspect according to a mark out of ten.

Skiing Conditions refers to the range of skiing on offer, the quality and efficiency of the lift installations, how accessible they are and how well they interlink, whether queues are a problem and whether the resort has access to the skiing areas of other resorts. If such is the case, the extent of the other resorts' skiing will also influence the mark that it obtains.

Snow Conditions are governed by the height of the resort (low ones will generally have poorer snow cover at either end of the season) and its top station, whether the slopes are north- or south-facing, and whether there are snow-making facilities. Due to climatic peculiarities, some low-lying resorts enjoy heavy snowfalls and a long season. Resorts with glacier skiing usually rate highly.

The three headings **For Beginners, For Intermediates** and **For Advanced Skiers** speak for themselves. Your standard of skiing should be a major consideration when selecting a resort, as nothing is more likely to guarantee a ruined holiday than finding yourself out of your depth if a less than expert skier or being obliged to trundle round easy slopes if you are looking for something to challenge your expertise. All resorts cater in some way for beginners; however, those that have attractive, snow-sure nursery slopes or a particularly good ski school will rate more highly.

Giving the full facts about children's facilities is especially difficult. A whole book could be written about skiing with children alone! The requirements of infant, five-, ten- or fifteen-year-old vary so enormously. Assuming that older children can be considered as adults in skiing terms, the **For Children** rating assesses a resort according to its facilities for the under-twelves, the provision of (or lack of) kindergartens both ski and non-ski, proximity and difficulty of lifts, whether there are discounts for children in ski school and on the lift pass, and if the resort is, in

general, a good place to take children. If a resort has special facilities for teenagers, it scores more highly.

For many, the **Après-Ski** is as important as the skiing. But for some, a night out can be as rewarding in a quiet hotel restaurant as in a raucous disco into the early hours. Nonetheless, the more lively the resort, the more it will score in this category, but you should also read the text carefully to be sure that the resort features the kind of après-ski you are looking for.

Non-skiers and the energetic also look to what else is on offer in a resort. **Other Sports** covers all the non-ski activities available, but also includes cross-country skiing.

Value for Money does not necessarily mean low prices. The criterion here is whether the goods or services are worth the price put upon them. Some resorts are notoriously overpriced: the cost of the lift pass does not reflect the skiing available or the hotels and bars charge excessively. Other resorts may have similar prices, but you get much more for your money.

A number of Berlitz **Skiers** (from one to five) has been attributed to each resort, in the same way as hotels are given star ratings. These represent the author's overall impression and are mainly based on how extensive the skiing and facilities are. You should look to the individual ratings and the general descriptions, however, in order to assess exactly how well suited the resort is to individual needs.

THE RESORTS AT A GLANCE

	Altitude (metres)	Top Station (metres)	No. of Lifts	Runs (kilometres)*	Skier Rating	Skiing Conditions	Snow Conditions	For Beginners	For Intermediates	For Advanced Skiers	For Children	Après-Ski	Other Sports	Value for Money
Adelboden	1400	2350	30	90	2	4	5	6	6	4	6	6	7	7
Andermatt	1447	2350	12	55	3	5	7	6	4	5	3	5	7	7
Anzère	1500	2420	12	40	3	5	7	4	7	5	3	6	7	7
Arosa	1800	2653	17	70	2+	4	6	6	7	5	6	6	7	7
Champéry	1050	2300	11	650	3	7	5	5	6	7	6	7	7	7
Champoussin	1550	2152	6	650	2	7	5	6	6	3	6	5	7	7
Château-d'Œx	1000	1800	12	50	2	4	4	4	6	3	5	6	7	7
Crans-Montana	1500	3000	40	160	4	7	5	4	7	6	5	6	7	7
Davos	1560	2844	40	320	4+	8	7	5	8	8	8	8	7	7
Les Diablerets	1200	2970	24	120	3+	7	7	6	8	6	8	7	7	7
Disentis	1150	2903	9	54	2	5	5	6	6	6	4	4	7	7
Engelberg	1050	3020	26	45	2+	4	4	6	4	4	6	5	7	7
Flims/Laax	1020	3018	34	220	3+	5	5	7	6	6	6	5	7	8
Grächen	1617	2870	14	40	2	6	6	7	5	5	5	5	7	5
Grindelwald	1050	2320	28	165§	3	7	4	8	6	7	7	8	7	7
Gstaad	1100	3000	14	250§	3	6	5	7	5	7	7	7	7	7

Resort															
Haute-Nendaz	1320	3328	32	320	2+	7	7	7	7	7	7	7	6	6	7
Klosters	1200	2844	26	320	4	8	6	6	7	8	6	6	7	7	7
Lenk	1068	2099	20	240	2	6	5	6	7	4	5	4	7	7	7
Lenzerheide-Valbella	1500	2865	37	155	2	6	5	6	7	5	6	6	6	6	7
Leysin	1200	2200	19	60	2+	6	5	6	7	4	6	7	7	7	7
Morgins	1400	2000	16	650	2	7	6	6	7	7	6	5	6	6	7
Mürren	1650	2970	8	50	2	6	7	6	6	7	6	5	5	7	7
Pontresina	1800	3304	12	350§	3+	6	5	6	6	5	6	7	7	7	7
Rougemont	1000	2186	2	50	2+	5	4	6	6	5	5	5	6	6	7
Saas-Fee	1800	3500	26	80	2	7	8	5	8	5	7	8	8	8	7
St. Moritz	1856	3304	26	350§	4	7	6	7	7	7	6	8	8	8	7
Verbier	1500	3330	36	320	4	9	8	8	8	6	9	8	8	7	7
Veysonnaz	1300	3304	35	320	5	7	6	6	7	5	5	4	7	5	7
Villars	1300	2120	24	120	2	7	5	6	6	6	6	7	8	7	7
Wengen	1274	2320	18	165§	4	7	5	6	7	7	6	8	8	7	7
Zermatt	1620	3820	37	150	5	9	8	5	8	9	8	9	8	8	7

* with linked resorts
§ on same lift pass, not necessarily linked by ski

ADELBODEN

Access: *Nearest airport*: Zurich (2½ hrs.); Bern (1 hr.). *By road*: N6 motorway, exit Spiez. *By rail*: to Bern, connection to Frutigen, then by bus.

Tourist Office: CH-3715 Adelboden. Tel. (033) 73 22 52

Altitude: 1400 m. *Top:* 2350 m.

Language: German

Beds: 10,000

Population: 3,400

Health: Doctors in resort. *Hospital:* Frutigen (15 km.)

Runs: 120 km. (240 km. with Lenk)

Lifts: 30 (50 with Lenk)

Ski areas: Engstligenalp, Boden, Schwandfeldspitz, Hahnenmoos

Ski schools: Schweizer Skischule Adelboden

Linked resorts: Lenk

Season: December to April

Kindergarten: *Non-ski*: from 1 year. *With ski*: 4–6 years.

Prices: *Lift pass*: 6 days Sfr. 162 (children Sfr. 97). *Ski school*: Group Sfr. 85 for 6 half-days; private Sfr. 38 per hour.

RATINGS

Skiing Conditions	Snow Conditions	For Beginners	For Intermediates	For Advanced Skiers	For Children	Après-Ski	Other Sports	Value for Money
4	5	6	6	4	6	6	7	7

ADELBODEN

THE RESORT

Adelboden, in the Engstligen valley of the Bernese Oberland, is one of the most charming Alpine villages in Switzerland. Dominated by the impressive Wildstrubel mountain, the resort is full of character, with lots of beautiful old wooden chalet buildings. It is a popular tourist destination in summer as well as winter. The skiing links with the neighbouring resort of Lenk, which has a rather different character.

THE SKIING

The problem with Adelboden's skiing is that there isn't a single ski area, but a collection of four separate areas linked only by road: at Geils/Hahnenmoos, Boden/Fleckli, Birg/Engstligenalp,

and Tschentenegg/Schwandfeldspitz. For all except the Tschentenegg area it is necessary to take a long walk or, normally, a bus from the centre of Adelboden. A car can be as much of a hindrance as a help, since the distances to be driven are relatively short, and parking at the bottom lift stations can often be a problem.

There is not much in the way of difficult skiing, but there are plenty of good, sunny slopes for intermediates. The Tschentenegg area rises up to the Schwandfeldspitz summit at 1938 m. and offers a solitary black run all the way back down to Adelboden.

The lifts from Boden up to the Höchsthorn (1903 m.) serve fairly easy runs, while the lift on the Fleckli system rises to 1861 m., offering more challenging skiing.

From Birg, a cable car goes to the top of the Engstligenalp (1964 m.), but you also have to return by this cable car, and the skiing offered by the drag lifts up here does not really justify the laborious journey.

Geils gives access to the most interesting and challenging skiing in the Adelboden region and also provides the link with Lenk. The best runs are those emanating from the top of the Laveygrat chair lift, at 2200 m.

APRÈS-SKI

Adelboden is not as quiet after dark as it sometimes seems. The illusion is created principally because most of the après-ski activity goes on inside hotels. The Alte Taverne in the Nevada-Palace Hotel is the largest and most exciting nightspot. However, this is a smart and rather formal hotel; those in search of cheaper, more informal nightlife should find it at the Hotel Kreuz, particularly in the pizzeria. There is also a cinema, with films in English.

OTHER ACTIVITIES

Cross-country skiers can enjoy 40 km. of tracks, and there are 40 km. of walks. Skating and curling take place on indoor and outdoor rinks, and there is swimming, riding, sleigh-rides, hang-gliding from the Schwandfeldspitz, and skibob. For a taste of local culture and history, call in at the Heimatmuseum.

ANDERMATT

Access: *Nearest airport:* Zurich (2 hrs.). *By road:* N2 motorway, exit Göschenen. *By rail:* to Göschenen, then Oberalp railway to Andermatt.

Tourist Office: CH-6490 Andermatt. Tel. (044) 6 74 54

Altitude: 1447 m. *Top:* 2963 m.

Language: German

Beds: 700 in hotels, 1,000 in apartments

Population: 1,450

Health: Doctors and military hospital in resort.
Hospital: Altdorf (37 km.)

Runs: 55 km.

Lifts: 12

Ski areas: Gemsstock, Nätschen-Stöckli

Ski schools: Schweizer Skischule Andermatt

Linked resorts: None

Season: December to April

Kindergarten: *Non-ski:* none. *With ski:* none, but ski school from 4 years.

Prices: *Lift pass:* 6 days Sfr. 149. *Ski school:* Group Sfr. 37 per day (children Sfr. 35); private Sfr. 43–48 per hour.

RATINGS

Skiing Conditions: 5
Snow Conditions: 7
For Beginners: 6
For Intermediates: 4
For Advanced Skiers: 7
For Children: 5
Après-Ski: 3
Other Sports: 5
Value for Money: 7

THE RESORT

Often described as being at the "crossroads of the Alps", the tiny, traditional village of Andermatt is the major ski resort in the small Swiss canton of Uri. The St. Gotthard Pass into Italy passes by Andermatt, which also lies between the Furka and Oberalp passes.

Andermatt is reminiscent of more famous Swiss resorts such as Zermatt and Saas-Fee, although it is much smaller and more compact than either of them. The resort is not car-free, but private vehicles tend to be discouraged, and the streets are narrow. (Weekends are the worst times for traffic and queues.)

THE SKIING

Andermatt has a reputation for having some of the most reliable snow conditions in Switzerland—it also gets more than its fair share of sun. (But it can be cold in the village after the sun goes down behind the mountains which hem it in.) The resort has some very demanding skiing on its principal ski area, the Gemsstock, rising up to almost 3000 m. There is plenty to please black-run-lovers, including the runs that come straight down the front of the Gemsstock.

Getting up this mountain tends to be rather less fun; there is a two-stage cable car for which there are often queues at peak times. The two other lifts on the Gemsstock—a chair lift and a drag—are relatively short, so the cable cars constitute the main means of getting back uphill.

The other principal ski area is Nätschen-Stöckli, at only 1842 m., which is reached from the opposite end of the village, either by a fairly new chair lift (which begins beside the army barracks) or by the traditional method, train to Nätschen station. There are a couple of good mountain restaurants at Nätschen, and

the runs down to Andermatt are mainly wide, easy and sunny; the exception is the black run underneath the chair lift.

The Andermatt lift pass also covers the installations in the neighbouring villages of Hospental and Realp, reached by road or rail. The former offers the better skiing—a chair lift followed by a drag lift ascending to 2661 m. Realp is really not of interest to anyone other than beginners.

Andermatt is a major centre for ski touring, and top guides like Martin Epp and Alex Clapasson are based here.

APRÈS-SKI

Eating and drinking take place mainly in hotels, but there is a disco, the Downhill, and a cinema showing English films.

OTHER ACTIVITIES

You'll find 20 km. of cross-country tracks, skating (outdoor), curling, tobogganing, sleigh-rides and bowling.

ANZÈRE

Access: *Nearest airport*: Geneva (3 hrs.). *By road*: N9 motorway, exit Sion, then direction Montana. *By rail*: to Sion, then by post bus. Tourist Office: CH-1972 Anzère. Tel. (027) 38 25 19

Altitude: 1500 m. *Top:* 2420 m.	Ski areas: Pas-de-Maimbré, Grillesse, Les Luys, Les Rousses, Le Bâté, Tsalan, Pralan, Duez, Le Chamossaire, Plan des Conches
Language: French	
Beds: 6,500	
Population: 400	
Health: Doctor in resort. *Hospital:* Sion (18 km.)	Ski schools: Ecole Suisse de Ski Anzère
Runs: 40 km.	Linked resorts: None
Lifts: 12	Season: Mid-December to Easter
	Kindergarten: *Non-ski*: 2–10 years. *With ski*: 4–12 years.

Prices: *Lift pass*: 6 days Sfr. 141 (children Sfr. 80–85). *Ski school*: Group Sfr. 19 for half-day (children Sfr. 17); private Sfr. 35 per hour.

RATINGS

Skiing Conditions	Snow Conditions	For Beginners	For Intermediates	For Advanced Skiers	For Children	Après-Ski	Other Sports	Value for Money
5	6	6	7	5	7	6	6	7

THE RESORT

Anzère is one of Switzerland's—indeed Europe's—most successful purpose-built ski resorts. Its greatest benefit is probably its beautiful south-facing position high above the Rhône valley, just to the west of Crans-Montana. Most of the accommodation and many of the pistes offer superb panoramic views of the Alps.

Architecturally, Anzère is a successful blend of large and small buildings in the traditional chalet style, and the sloping roofs help the resort to nestle into the hillside. The centre of the resort is relatively compact and car-free. Unusually for a purpose-built resort, there is a real village atmosphere, and the locals genuinely care about the visitors, making this a particularly popular resort for families, many of whom return year after year to self-catering accommodation.

THE SKIING

The Anzère ski area appeals more to intermediate skiers who appreciate skiing on pretty, sunny slopes than to experts who demand consistently challenging terrain. This helps to explain its special suitability for family groups of mixed skiing ability. Most of the skiing is up above the tree line (it rises to a height of 2420 m. from a village level of 1500 m.) and there is a good snow record, especially considering its south-facing aspect.

There are two main routes from the resort into the ski area: the Pas-de-Maimbré télécabine, for which there can be queues at peak times, and the Pralan-Tsalan chair lift. The long run down Combe de Serin to Les Rousses is one of the most pleasant here, bringing you to the best mountain restaurant in the area. The run from Pas-de-Maimbré to Anzère itself can be quite taxing at times, particularly the last, wooded section to the resort itself.

APRÈS-SKI

What is basically a quiet, family-oriented resort cannot be expected to offer a tremendous amount of nightlife, but nevertheless Anzère has three discos, all situated in hotels: the Zodiaque, the Masques and de la Poste. The Zodiaque and Eden hotels also have piano bars. There are about 15 restaurants in the resort, ranging from pizzerias and crêperies to more serious establishments like le Grenier, the Gros Roc and the restaurant of the Hotel des Masques.

OTHER ACTIVITIES

Anzère offers 15 km. of cross-country tracks and 12 km. of walking paths, skating, bowling, curling, swimming and para-gliding. There is also a small Alpine museum, and trips down to the valley town of Sion are possible.

AROSA

Access: *Nearest airport*: Zurich (2½ hrs.). *By road*: N13 motorway, exit Chur-Nord. *By rail*: international express to Chur, then by Rhaetian railway to Arosa.

Tourist Office: CH-7050 Arosa. Tel. (081) 31 16 21

Altitude: 1800 m. *Top:* 2653 m.	Ski areas: Brüggerhorn, Weisshorn, Plattenhorn, Hörnli, Tschuggen
Language: German	
Beds: 12,000	Ski schools: Schweizer Skischule Arosa
Population: 2,700	
Health: Doctors, dentists and fracture clinic in resort. *Hospital:* Chur (30 km.)	Linked resorts: None
	Season: December to April
Runs: 70 km.	Kindergarten: *Non-ski*: 3–8 years. *With ski*: from 2½ years.
Lifts: 17	

Prices: *Lift pass*: 6 days Sfr. 145 (children Sfr. 101). *Ski school*: Group Sfr. 145 for 6 days (children Sfr. 130); private Sfr. 40 per hour.

RATINGS: Skiing Conditions 4 / Snow Conditions 5 / For Beginners 6 / For Intermediates 6 / For Advanced Skiers 4 / For Children 6 / Après-Ski 7 / Other Sports 7 / Value for Money 7

THE RESORT

Arosa is one of those classic, old-fashioned ski resorts that could only be found in Switzerland. A village has existed on this site at the top of the Schanfigg Valley, close to Chur in the Grisons canton, since the 13th century. The Arosa Ski Club was founded in 1903, but the ski school was not established until 30 years later,

and the first three lifts were built in 1938. Accommodation is mostly in hotels, of which there is a great variety, ranging from the very grand to the very simple.

Arosa is an ideal resort for mixed groups of holiday-makers, which include non-skiers as well as skiers. Indeed, statistics show that half the winter visitors to Arosa do not ski. And the variety of non-skiing activities is such that they are unlikely to get bored.

THE SKIING

Arosa is certainly a resort for beginners and intermediate skiers rather than for experts. It is a beautiful place in which to learn and become proficient in basic skills before tackling a more demanding resort. Arosa itself is fairly high up at 1800 m., and the skiing stretches up to 2653 m., almost all of it above the tree line. Although there are less than 20 lifts, they are well laid out, and there are some good long, broad runs.

The Weisshorn is the highest point in the area, from which the most difficult run—a taxing black to Carmennahütte—begins. Others down from here are of intermediate standard, unless you happen to be an experienced off-piste skier in the company of a local guide, in which case there is further variety to be explored.

The Hörnli sector of the Arosa ski area rises to 2512 m. and offers wide, sunny pistes perfectly suited to the early intermediate skier. There is also an off-piste descent from here which will take you all the way to the nearby resort of Lenzerheide. The nicest mountain restaurant in the area, at the top of the Hörnligrat, has a sunny terrace.

APRÈS-SKI

With so many non-skiers in the resort, there are always plenty of people with energy for après-ski (or, technically, après-non-ski) activities. Nevertheless, the average age of the clientele is older

than in resorts with more demanding skiing. The most popular centre for nightlife is the Kursaal, which has a variety of bars and restaurants, including a reasonably up-to-date disco and a cinema.

With so many hotels in the resort, it is not surprising that much of the après-ski revolves around them. The much-loved bar of the Arosa Kulm Hotel was transplanted from the 1929 version of the same hotel after it was rebuilt in 1975. The Hotel Park is fairly lively and boasts a bowling alley, while the Tschuggen Grand Hotel is a good place for more traditional dancing.

OTHER ACTIVITIES

Arosa offers 30 km. of cross-country tracks, more than 30 km. of paths for walkers, skating (artificial and natural rinks), curling, squash, indoor tennis, sleigh-rides, indoor golf, horse riding, swimming, bowling, tobogganing and skibob. There are weekly concerts, exhibitions and a regional museum at Innerarosa, open twice a week.

CHAMPÉRY

Access: *Nearest airport*: Geneva (1½–2 hrs.). *By road*: N9 motorway, exit Aigle or Bex. *By rail*: to Aigle, then mountain railway (AOMC) to Champéry.
Tourist Office: CH-1874 Champéry. Tel. (025) 79 11 41

Altitude: 1050 m. *Top:* 2300 m.	Ski areas: Planachaux
Language: French	Ski schools: Ecole Suisse de Ski Champéry
Beds: 7,300	Linked resorts: Portes du Soleil resorts
Population: 1,000	
Health: Doctors in resort. *Hospital:* Monthey (14 km.)	Season: December to April
Runs: 650 km. in Portes du Soleil area	Kindergarten: *Non-ski*: one month–7 years. *With ski*: from 3 years.
Lifts: 11 (220 in Portes du Soleil area)	

Prices: *Lift pass*: 6 days Sfr. 165 (children Sfr. 116). *Ski school*: Group Sfr. 17 for half-day (children Sfr. 16); private Sfr. 35 per hour.

RATINGS

Skiing Conditions	Snow Conditions	For Beginners	For Intermediates	For Advanced Skiers	For Children	Après-Ski	Other Sports	Value for Money
7	5	5	7	6	6	6	6	7

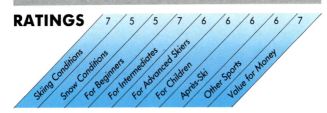

THE RESORT

Champéry is the key Swiss resort in the ski area known as the Portes du Soleil, straddling the Franco-Swiss border. (Avoriaz, Morzine and Châtel are some of the more famous French resorts in this complex of more than a dozen stations of varying sizes.)

Champéry was a ski resort long before the Portes du Soleil concept was invented, and until recently its ancient cable car forcibly reminded you of the fact. What is more, Champéry is a pretty year-round mountain village with a great deal of character. Its proximity to Geneva is a mixed blessing: short transfer times, but bad queues at weekends and holidays.

THE SKIING

The Portes du Soleil is nowadays claiming to be the biggest ski area in Europe, but since the "3 Vallées" in France, which has long claimed to be the biggest ski area in the world, is also in Europe, things are getting a trifle confusing. It all depends on how you measure a ski area. The Portes du Soleil is a very different kind of interlinked area from the 3 Vallées. In the 3 Vallées, you systematically move from one valley to the next via a well-connected lift system. The Portes du Soleil area is, by contract, a much looser affiliation of a greater number of resorts in many different valleys. It is possible to get from each resort to every other resort, but sometimes the route will be very tortuous and time-consuming.

It is impossible here to describe the whole expanse of skiing on offer in the Portes du Soleil area. Obviously there is an enormous amount of it and there are runs to suit skiers of all standards. If the area has a centre, then it is Avoriaz, the purpose-built French resort which, at a height of 1800 m., is also the highest resort in the region. Champéry itself is a relatively low resort at only 1050 m. and consequently is not a good bet for early- or late-season skiing.

The runs down from Avoriaz towards Champéry include the most famous run in the whole Portes du Soleil area: "The Wall" or "The Swiss Wall" at Chavanette. A very steep and mogul-ridden slope, its precise difficulty depends on the snow conditions and how unpleasantly the moguls have been carved up. For most skiers it is the kind of run that gives satisfaction when you have got down it, but only real experts can claim to derive pleasure during the actual descent. (Many quite competent skiers choose to descend by chair lift.)

There is masses of wide-open, easy, sunny skiing on the Champéry side, stretching down to the neighbouring (Swiss) resort of Les Crosets and including the Planachaux area. Irritatingly, the runs back down to Champéry do not come back to the centre of the resort, but to one end. However, there is a bus service covering the final stretch into the middle of the village.

Although mountain restaurants are nothing special in this area, the Swiss ones tend to be of better quality than the French ones. If you intend to lunch in France, it pays to take the right currency rather than be subjected to a rip-off exchange rate.

APRÈS-SKI

Champéry is not the most exciting resort in Switzerland as far as après-ski is concerned. The main meeting place after skiing is Le Pub, particularly popular with the British. Le Farinet is a rather more sophisticated spot for eating, drinking and dancing. The best restaurants are mostly in hotels: Le Mazot in the Hotel de Champéry, the Victor Hugo in the Hotel Suisse, and the Vieux Chalet in the Beau Séjour for fondues and raclettes.

OTHER ACTIVITIES

For cross-country skiers there is an 8-km. track, and 15 km. of walks, swimming in indoor pools, skating, curling, ice hockey, and a fitness centre are also available.

CHAMPOUSSIN

Access: *Nearest airport:* Geneva (1½–2 hrs.). *By road:* N9 motorway, exit Aigle or Saint-Triphon. *By rail:* international connections to Aigle, then AOMC railway.

Tourist Office: CH-1873 Val-d'Illiez. Tel. (025) 77 27 27

Altitude: 1550 m. *Top:* 2152 m.	Lifts: 6 (220 in Portes du Soleil area)
Language: French	
Beds: 800	Ski areas: Pointe de l'Au
Population: 10	Ski schools: Ecole Suisse de Ski Val-d'Illiez
Health: Doctors in Champéry and Troistorrents. *Hospital:* Monthey (13 km.)	Linked resorts: Portes du Soleil resorts
Runs: 650 km. in Portes du Soleil area	Season: December to April
	Kindergarten: None

Prices: *Lift pass:* 6 days Sfr. 165 (children Sfr. 116). *Ski school:* Group Sfr. 17 for half-day (children Sfr. 16); private Sfr. 35 per hour.

RATINGS

Skiing Conditions	Snow Conditions	For Beginners	For Intermediates	For Advanced Skiers	For Children	Après-Ski	Other Sports	Value for Money
7	5	6	7	6	6	3	5	7

For map see pp. 40–41.

THE RESORT

Champoussin is a small purpose-built resort on the Swiss side of the Franco-Swiss Portes du Soleil ski area. The resort consists largely of apartment blocks, but these have been constructed sympathetically in giant chalet style.

Champoussin is situated in the Val-d'Illiez, gets a fair amount of sunshine and has beautiful views. It is an ideal resort for families or other groups on self-catering holidays.

THE SKIING

The neighbouring resorts of Champéry and Les Crosets are easily reached by ski from Champoussin, but an alternative ski route in the opposite direction takes you over to Morgins. From

Morgins it is possible to continue on the Portes du Soleil circuit by going up and over to Châtel, where you find yourself in the French sector of this vast area.

The lifts from Champoussin to Morgins and Châtel are mostly drag lifts (there are also occasional chair lifts), and the runs involved are easily accomplished by intermediate skiers, as indeed are the great majority of runs in the Portes du Soleil. There is very pleasant skiing through the trees on the way down to Morgins.

In the opposite direction two chair lifts carry skiers out of Champoussin and up to the Pointe de l'Au, above an enjoyable advanced/intermediate mogul field, from where one skis down to Les Crosets. From here there are essentially two main routes over to Avoriaz in France. The most direct is to take the télécabine up to the Pointe de Mossette, down a long red run to the hamlet of Les Brocheaux, from where a chair lift runs up to Avoriaz itself. The alternative is to take a lift from the far side of Les Crosets and work your way across to the Pas de Chavanette, taking a chair lift up the notorious Chavanette or "Swiss Wall" steep mogul-field and then skiing down all the way to Avoriaz itself. (The only problem about this chair-lift ride is that it may make you even more nervous about negotiating the "Swiss Wall" on your way home. But remember that even rather good skiers prefer to take the chair lift down.)

APRÈS-SKI

Champoussin is a quiet family resort that does not have a great deal to offer in the way of nightlife. The resort's principal hotel, the Alpage, is probably the major nocturnal focal point. The best food is also usually to be found here, but Le Poussin is good for cheese dishes and crêpes. Champoussin also boasts a disco and a couple of bars.

OTHER ACTIVITIES

A small cross-country loop and some paths for walking are available, as well as skating, curling, swimming (in Hotel Alpage) and tobogganing. Para-gliding and hang-gliding are the more adventurous sports on offer.

CHÂTEAU-D'ŒX

Access: *Nearest airport*: Geneva (2 hrs.). *By road*: N12 motorway, exit Bulle, then via Montbovon. *By rail*: to Montreux, then Montreux-Oberland-Bernois (MOB) railway to Château-d'Œx.
Tourist Office: CH-1837 Château-d'Œx. Tel. (029) 4 77 88

Altitude: 1000 m. *Top:* 1800 m.	Ski areas: La Braye, Les Monts Chevreuils
Language: French	
Beds: 4,000	Ski schools: Ecole Suisse de Ski Château-d'Œx
Population: 3,000	
Health: Doctors, dentists and hospital in resort	Linked resorts: None
	Season: December to April
Runs: 50 km.	Kindergarten: *Non-ski*: 1–4 years. *With ski*: 2–7 years.
Lifts: 12	

Prices: *Lift pass*: 6 days Sfr. 126 (children Sfr. 75). *Ski school*: Group Sfr. 17 for half-day (children Sfr. 15); private Sfr. 40 per hour.

RATINGS

Skiing Conditions	Snow Conditions	For Beginners	For Intermediates	For Advanced Skiers	For Children	Après-Ski	Other Sports	Value for Money
4	4	4	6	5	6	5	7	7

For map see pp. 90–91.

CHÂTEAU-D'ŒX

THE RESORT

A traditional Alpine farming village first and a ski resort second, Château-d'Œx is part of the White Highlands ski area, lately renamed, to this resort's displeasure, the Gstaad Superski Region. It is nowadays most famous for its Alpine hot-air ballooning festival which takes place every year towards the end of January. In good weather the most spectacular sights are the mass ascents when over 50 balloons take to the skies simultaneously.

THE SKIING

Frankly, if you wish to do much skiing from a base in Château-d'Œx, then you need to have the use of a car. There are public transport systems—mostly railways—and these are generally included on the lift pass, but getting from one resort to another by this method is tiresome: a car is so much easier.

Château-d'Œx does not have an enormous amount of skiing to offer. (The resort itself is actually fairly low at only 1000 m.) There is a cable car which takes skiers up to 1225 m., from where a télécabine runs up to the top of La Braye, itself only 1630 m. high, where there are some easy drag lifts. Often it is necessary to take the cable car back down to the resort because of lack of snow on runs to resort level. In any case these runs terminate with a bus ride back to the resort itself.

Rougemont is the closest resort offering really good skiing, with a two-stage télécabine giving access to the demanding slopes of the Videmanette. (The most challenging slope of all, the run down the front, is often closed.)

Going further afield, other resorts within range of Château-d'Œx include Gstaad, with its three separate ski areas, Saanenmöser and Zweisimmen. Les Diablerets and even Villars are not that far away, but these areas do require a separate lift pass.

APRÈS-SKI

Château-d'Œx is quite a jolly little village, and for après-ski activities the visitors mix very much with the locals. The pub below the village hall is a popular meeting place, but it can become unpleasantly crowded. By far the most appealing après-ski venue is the Bon Accueil. This hotel, in a large chalet-style building, dates back to 1756. The only drawback is that it is a steep uphill walk from the village, but taxis are available. There is a good restaurant here, but the nicest part of all is the cosy cellar bar, where a log fire burns and you can relax in comfortable armchairs. For those wanting to eat the traditional specialities of the region, the Taverne of the Beau-Séjour is worth a visit.

OTHER ACTIVITIES

In Château-d'Œx, there are 30 km. of cross-country tracks, plus skating, curling, indoor and outdoor horse riding, hot-air balloon rides, skibob and tobogganing. Other interesting diversions include a folk museum and the cheese farm, where you can watch the traditional methods by which the local cheeses are made.

CRANS-MONTANA

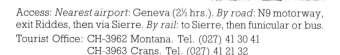

Access: *Nearest airport*: Geneva (2½ hrs.). *By road*: N9 motorway, exit Riddes, then via Sierre. *By rail*: to Sierre, then funicular or bus.
Tourist Office: CH-3962 Montana. Tel. (027) 41 30 41
CH-3963 Crans. Tel. (027) 41 21 32

Altitude: 1500 m. *Top*: 3000 m.	Ski areas: Aminona/Petit Bonvin, Cry d'Err/Bella Lui, Les Violettes/Plaine Morte, Chetzeron
Language: French	
Beds: 30,000	
Population: 4,500	Ski schools: Ecole Suisse de Ski Montana, Ecole Suisse de Ski Crans
Health: Doctors, dentists and fracture clinic in resort. *Hospital:* Sierre (15 km.)	
	Linked resorts: None
	Season: December to April; summer skiing on glacier
Runs: 160 km.	
Lifts: 40	Kindergarten: *Non-ski*: 2 months–12 years. *With ski*: 3–7 years.

Prices: *Lift pass*: 6 days Sfr. 164 (children Sfr. 98). *Ski school*: 6 days Sfr. 90 (children Sfr. 75); private Sfr. 40 for 50 min.

RATINGS

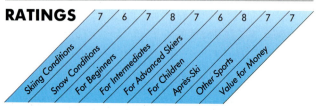

Skiing Conditions	Snow Conditions	For Beginners	For Intermediates	For Advanced Skiers	For Children	Après-Ski	Other Sports	Value for Money
7	6	7	8	7	6	8	7	7

THE RESORT

Situated on a south-facing plateau above Sierre in the Rhône valley, Crans-Montana is the sunniest resort in Switzerland. Historically Crans and Montana were two separate resorts that sprawled into each other, but they have now officially amalgamated. However, each retains its distinctive character, Crans being undoubtedly the more up-market of the two, with expensive boutiques and many fur coats in evidence.

THE SKIING

Crans-Montana was the venue for the 1987 World Ski Championships, and new lift facilities—and even new pistes—installed for this event have greatly improved the skiing possibilities here. Essentially the ski area is a mini "3 Valleys" complex. These are: Cry d'Err/Bella Lui, Les Violettes/Plaine Morte and Aminona/Petit Bonvin. Access to the system is provided at four points along the plateau: Crans, Montana, Les Barzettes and Aminona. All these bottom stations are linked by a free shuttle bus service.

Crans-Montana has masses of fine intermediate skiing, but it also offers a good number of taxing runs for the expert. These include the mogul-ridden slopes below the Bella Lui summit, the top section of the Piste Nationale downhill course, the run down from Plaine Morte and the steep mogul slopes beside the Toula lift.

There are spectacular panoramic views from the top of the Plaine Morte glacier (3000 m.), and the run down offers a perfect combination of great skiing and superb scenery. A limited amount of easy summer skiing is available on the Plaine Morte glacier itself. The only problem with this sector is that it is often closed during severe weather or after heavy snowfalls, and in high season there can be longish queues for the cable car.

Because so many of its slopes are south-facing, Crans-Montana suffers from poor snow cover and icy runs, particularly lower down, at either end of the season. The most atmospheric mountain restaurant is at Merbé, between Cry d'Err and Grand Signal, but the more modern restaurants at Les Violettes and Plaine Morte serve good food.

APRÈS-SKI

Tea-rooms are popular après-ski rendezvous points, and among the best are the Constellation in Crans and Gerber in Montana. The hotel bars are fashionable but expensive; the bar of the Crans-Ambassador is usually well patronized. But there are cheaper drinking places in the form of La Grange in Montana and Le Pub in Crans. Au Gréni in Montana is one of the best restaurants specializing in Valaisan fare, while Au Vieux Moulin (Montana) is a good pizzeria. There is no shortage of smart nightclubs, those in Crans being generally more expensive than those in Montana. Crans has a cinema.

OTHER ACTIVITIES

You'll find 40 km. of cross-country tracks, skating, curling, swimming (hotel pools and spa swimming pool), tennis, bowling, squash, horse riding, 50 km. of marked walks, tobogganing, skibob, fitness centres, indoor golf and hot-air ballooning.

DAVOS

 +

Access: *Nearest airport*: Zurich (3 hrs.). *By road*: N3 motorway, exit Landquart, then via Klosters. *By rail*: station in resort (on Zurich-Landquart-Davos railway).

Tourist Office: CH-7270 Davos. Tel. (083) 3 51 35

Altitude: 1560 m. *Top:* 2844 m.	Ski areas: Schatzalp/Strela, Parsenn, Jakobshorn, Pischa, Rinerhorn, Gotschna, Madrisa
Language: German	
Beds: 6,500 in hotels, 14,000 in apartments	Ski schools: Schweizer Skischule Davos Platz, Schweizer Skischule Davos Dorf
Population: 12,600	
Health: Doctors, dentists and hospital in resort.	Linked resorts: Klosters
Runs: 180 km. (320 with Klosters)	Season: December to mid-April
Lifts: 40 (55 with Klosters)	Kindergarten: *Non-ski*: for all ages (baby-sitting facilities for infants). *With ski*: 3–10 years.

Prices: *Lift pass*: 6 days Sfr. 190 (children Sfr. 142). *Ski school*: Group Sfr. 20 for half-day; private Sfr. 40 per hour.

RATINGS

Skiing Conditions	Snow Conditions	For Beginners	For Intermediates	For Advanced Skiers	For Children	Après-Ski	Other Sports	Value for Money
8	7	5	8	8	5	8	8	7

THE RESORT

Davos is no pretty little Alpine village. To be honest, it is a rather large, ugly flat-roofed town. At 1560 m. it boasts of being the highest town in Europe and the views up out of the town towards the mountains are impressive. Because Davos has a life apart from skiing (it is a major year-round international conference centre), it offers a range of facilities you would not normally find in a ski resort.

THE SKIING

The various ski areas of the Davos region are not well interlinked, but because they are in different situations, you are always likely to find good conditions in at least one of them.

The main ski area at Davos is the Parsenn region, which links with the Schatzalp/Strelagrat sector to the west and the Klosters/Gotschnagrat sector to the east. This is a popular area for intermediate and advanced skiers. There are plenty of broad,

open pistes, as well as some challenging mogul slopes. The most remarkable of these runs is down from the top of the Weissfluhgipfel (2844 m.).

The Schatzalp area is relatively quiet and, as it is rarely pisted, offers an appealing natural mogul field. The new Schiferbahn télécabine makes returning from the Klosters ski area much easier, so Davos-based skiers can easily experience the delights of the wooden Schwendi mountain restaurants. In good snow conditions, really adventurous skiers can ski one of the longest runs in Europe, all the way from the top of the Weissfluhgipfel to Küblis in the valley (813 m.) and then take the narrow-gauge Rhaetian railway back to Davos.

The Jakobshorn area rises up from Davos Platz and offers good mogul runs, as well as some excellent off-piste areas round the back of the mountain. Rinerhorn is a small north-facing mountain about ten minutes' train ride (included on REGA lift pass) from Davos. It is good for powder and off-piste skiing. Because it is out of town, Rinerhorn is a good place to go when the main resort is crowded, as it often is at weekends. The other Davos ski area is at Pischa, a short free bus ride from the Parsenn lift. This is mainly suited to intermediates, unless you have a guide to show you the off-piste possibilities.

APRÈS-SKI

There is nothing cosy or rustic about après-ski in Davos: this is a sophisticated town. The Pöstli Corner bar of the Posthotel Morosani is always popular after skiing, as is the Chämi bar with its surreal decor. The Davoserhof has the finest hotel restaurant, while the Gentiana is a good place for fondues. The Padrino pizzeria is a useful place for a cheap meal. Chinese restaurants flourish here—the newest and smartest is the Zauberberg in the

lavishly refurbished Hotel Europe. The Pöstli Club in the Posthotel and the Cabanna Club (also in the Europe) are the most popular nightclubs, but there are many others. The two cinemas show films in English.

OTHER ACTIVITIES

Davos is immensely proud of its 4-km. floodlit cross-country track. There are a further 75 km. of trails in the area, as well as 60 km. of cleared walks. The resort also offers skating (on the largest natural ice rink in Europe) and curling, swimming, horse riding and hang-gliding, para-gliding, tennis, squash, bowling, tobogganing and sleigh-rides. Excursions can be made to St. Moritz and Chur.

LES DIABLERETS

Access: *Nearest airport*: Geneva (2 hrs.). *By road*: N9 motorway, exit Aigle. *By rail*: station in resort.
Tourist Office: CH-1865 Les Diablerets. Tel. (025) 53 13 58

Altitude: 1200 m. *Top:* 2970 m.

Language: French

Beds: 900 in hotels, 2,000 in chalets and apartments

Population: 1,200

Health: Doctors in resort. *Hospital:* Aigle (19 km.)

Runs: 60 km. (120 with Villars)

Lifts: 24 (48 with Villars)

Ski areas: Isenau, Meilleret, Glacier

Ski schools: Ecole Suisse de Ski Les Diablerets

Linked resorts: Villars

Season: December to April; summer skiing on glacier

Kindergarten: *Non-ski*: 1–5 years. *With ski*: 2–11 years.

Prices: *Lift pass:* 6 days Sfr. 154 (children Sfr. 108). *Ski school*: Group Sfr. 17 for half-day (children Sfr. 16); private Sfr. 40 per hour.

RATINGS — Skiing Conditions 7 / Snow Conditions 7 / For Beginners 6 / For Intermediates 7 / For Advanced Skiers 6 / For Children 5 / Après-Ski 8 / Other Sports 7 / Value for Money 7

THE RESORT

Lying above the valley town of Aigle in the canton of Vaud, Les Diablerets is basically quite a pretty, old-fashioned mountain village, cleverly incorporating a number of large new chalet-style buildings (hotels and apartment blocks) without losing any of the atmosphere. Surrounded by high mountain peaks, including the Diablerets glacier itself, the resort is dramatically situated. The disadvantage of its position is that it is not particularly sunny, especially in the early part of winter. Although it is a small ski

resort, Diablerets is fairly smart, and the quality and variety of accommodation and après-ski entertainment reflects this. The village itself is quite low, so skiing down to resort level at either end of the season is not always possible.

THE SKIING

The much-publicized Diablerets glacier ski area is in fact principally intended for summer skiing. It is often closed in December and January because of bad weather. However, in the case of poor snow cover lower down, the glacier will sometimes open up to ensure that there is at least some skiing available. Even later in the season, the glacier can often be closed for days on end due to bad weather and/or avalanche danger. Another drawback is that the lifts on the glacier are not included on the general lift pass: a supplementary pass must be purchased.

Apart from the glacier, the Diablerets ski region consists of two other areas: Isenau and Meilleret, the latter rising to 1949 m., where it connects with the Villars lift system. This liaison is not perfect and involves quite a bit of poling and plodding. There are some reasonably challenging red runs on the Meilleret side, some going down to Les Diablerets itself and others going down to Vers l'Eglise along the valley.

The Isenau area, which rises to Floriettaz at 2120 m., offers very easy, pleasant skiing. From here you can link into the glacier area via the Pillon-Pierres Pointes télécabine. (Isenau itself is reached by télécabine from the centre of Les Diablerets.) When the glacier is open there are some good, challenging runs round the back of the Oldenhorn, as well as down from Cabane to Oldenegg. The highest point on the glacier ski area is Scex-Rouge at 2970 m.

APRÈS-SKI

Après-ski facilities in Les Diablerets are surprisingly impressive for a resort of this size. The best discos are at the Eurotel and the Ermitage (Le Refuge). The Ermitage also boasts an English pub, but those in search of a more genuine Swiss atmosphere should head for the Auberge de la Poste, which is one of the resort's older buildings, where traditional Swiss dishes such as raclette and fondue are served. Les Lilas is a rustic-style restaurant, while the Locanda Livia is good for pizzas and pasta.

OTHER ACTIVITIES

In the resort there are 25 km. of cross-country tracks, 20 km. of prepared walks, skating, curling, swimming, horse riding and tobogganing. Excursions down to Lake Geneva (Lac Léman) and the towns on its banks like Montreux and Vevey are quite feasible. Take the train down to Aigle and change.

DISENTIS

Access: *Nearest airport*: Zurich (2 hrs.). *By road*: N13 motorway, exit Reichenau, then direction Ilanz. *By rail*: express to Chur, connection to Disentis.
Tourist Office: CH-7180 Disentis. Tel. (086) 7 58 22

Altitude: 1150 m. *Top:* 2903 m.

Language: Romansh, German

Beds: 4,300

Population: 2,500

Health: Doctors in resort. *Hospital:* Ilanz (30 km.)

Runs: 54 km.

Lifts: 9

Ski areas: Péz Ault

Ski schools: Scola da Skis Svizra Disentis

Linked resorts: Sedrun

Season: December to April

Kindergarten: *Non-ski*: none. *With ski*: none, but ski school from 4 years.

Prices: *Lift pass*: 6 days Sfr. 131 (children Sfr. 105). *Ski school*: Group Sfr. 19 for half-day (children Sfr. 17); private Sfr. 45 per hour.

RATINGS

Skiing Conditions	Snow Conditions	For Beginners	For Intermediates	For Advanced Skiers	For Children	Après-Ski	Other Sports	Value for Money
4	5	6	6	4	6	4	7	7

THE RESORT

Disentis has been a ski resort only since 1971, when the main cable car was built. But for centuries it has been an important village on account of the Benedictine monastery (founded 765) and its beautiful baroque church, built around 1700. Don't get a hotel too near it—you won't sleep a wink for the noise of the clock chiming each quarter! Almost all of the hotels in Disentis have been constructed since 1971 and the result is a new purpose-built ski resort with an ancient heart and a real sense of community.

THE SKIING

Disentis is not by any means one of Switzerland's great ski resorts, but its combination of one cable car, a three-man chair lift and six drag lifts do give a respectable amount of skiing. The longest descent is a remarkable 12 km. from 2903 m., just below Péz Ault, right down to the bottom station which is at 1215 m.

The resort declines to grade its runs according to degrees of difficulty, but the skiing is mostly of intermediate standard, although the runs beside the Péz Ault and Gendusas Dadens lifts are more taxing than average. There are a number of interesting off-piste runs leading down from Péz Ault to the valley. The bottom station of the cable car is some distance out of the village;

there are one or two hotels close to it, but most skiers need to use the local shuttle bus. For those with cars or who like to take the narrow-gauge Furka-Oberalp or Rhätische-Bahn railways, Disentis is a good centre for day trips to neighbouring resorts like Flims/Laax and Andermatt.

APRÈS-SKI

Disentis is basically a family resort and things are pretty quiet after dark. What little entertainment there is goes on inside hotels. The Parkhotel Baur, just by the lift station, has an agreeable but unsophisticated nightclub called the Viva.

OTHER ACTIVITIES

Disentis has christened itself the "Wimbledon of the Alps" because it has the only grass tennis court in Switzerland. In winter, however, there are two indoor courts, as well as a well-equipped sports centre. This is also an ideal resort for the cross-country skier: one of the trails leads to the neighbouring village of Sedrun and takes around 2½ hours to complete—the return is by rail. Other facilities include: 16 km. of walks, skating, curling, swimming, fitness centre, sleigh-rides and para-gliding instruction.

ENGELBERG

Access: *Nearest airport*: Zurich (1½ hrs.). *By road*: N2 motorway, exit Stans-Süd. *By rail*: to Lucerne, then Lucerne-Stans-Engelberg railway.

Tourist Office: CH-6390 Engelberg. Tel. (041) 94 11 61

Altitude: 1050 m. *Top*: 3020 m.

Language: German

Beds: 2,160 in hotels, 4,580 in chalets and apartments

Population: 3,300

Health: Doctors in resort. *Hospital:* Stans (21 km.)

Runs: 45 km.

Lifts: 26

Ski areas: Brunni, Titlis-Trübsee, Jochpass, Engstlenalp, Jochstock, Gerschnialp

Ski schools: Schweizer Skischule Engelberg-Titlis, Neue Skischule Engelberg-Titlis

Linked resorts: None

Season: December to mid-April; summer skiing at Klein-Titlis

Kindergarten: *Non-ski*: 3–6 years. *With ski*: 3–6 years.

Prices: *Lift pass*: 6 days Sfr. 162 (children Sfr. 99). *Ski school*: Group Sfr. 41 per day; private Sfr. 42 per hour.

RATINGS

Skiing Conditions	Snow Conditions	For Beginners	For Intermediates	For Advanced Skiers	For Children	Après-Ski	Other Sports	Value for Money
5	5	5	6	6	6	7	7	7

THE RESORT

Engelberg, close to Lucerne in central Switzerland, is one of those ski resorts which possesses a real sense of tradition. This is hardly surprising since there has been a settlement on this site for centuries. A Benedictine abbey was first founded in 1120, but was burned down three times. The present building dates back to 1730. The resort is dominated by the remarkable Titlis mountain (3239 m.), and although the village itself is only 1050 m. high, it has a good snow-holding record.

THE SKIING

Engelberg has two main ski areas on opposite sides of the valley. The Brunni area rises up to Schönegg at 2040 m., while Trübsee culminates at 3020 m., just below the Titlis peak.

The lifts on the Brunni side run from the village itself and provide access to sunny, intermediate cruising slopes which run through woodland towards the end.

The more challenging skiing in the Engelberg area is on the Trübsee/Titlis side, but it is tiresome to reach. A bus or a long walk from the centre of the village takes you to the start of the lift system. Either the combination of a funicular railway and a cable car, or a recently constructed two-stage télécabine carries you up to Trübsee (1800 m.). The new télécabine has largely alleviated what used to be a very major queueing problem, although queues are

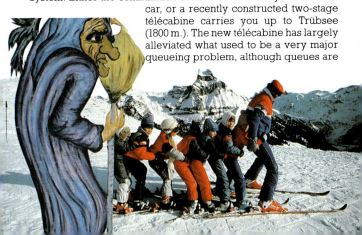

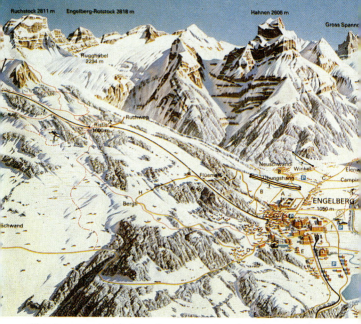

still to be expected in Engelberg at weekends and peak holiday periods.

From Trübsee a two-stage cable-car runs up to Stand (2450 m.) and then on to Klein-Titlis. There is one drag lift and the opportunity for some summer skiing up here, but in winter the only run down from Klein-Titlis to Stand is black, so all but expert skiers tend to travel up only as far as Stand itself. The runs down from Stand to Trübsee are all pleasant intermediate cruising.

APRÈS-SKI

The après-ski scene in Engelberg is by no means one of the liveliest in the Alps, but there is a good variety of restaurants, bars, cafés and discos to cater for all tastes and pockets, not to

mention a cinema. As in so many traditional Swiss resorts, much of the activity at night takes place inside hotels: the Ring-Hotel and the Bellevue-Terminus are among the larger establishments. The restaurant of the Hotel Hess is the finest in town and serves excellent *rösti*.

OTHER ACTIVITIES

In Engelberg you can take advantage of 35 km. of cross-country tracks, 35 km. of paths for walking, skating, curling, swimming, indoor tennis, tobogganing and sleigh-rides. You can visit the abbey (Monday to Friday) or take an excursion down to the delightful town of Lucerne, tour its historic sights or cruise on its lake in an old-world paddlesteamer.

FLIMS/LAAX

Access: *Nearest airport*: Zurich (2 hrs.). *By road*: N13 motorway, exit Chur, then direction Flims. *By rail*: to Chur, then by post bus.
Tourist Office: CH-7031 Laax 1. Tel. (086) 3 43 43
Tourist Office: CH-7018 Flims Waldhaus. Tel. (081) 39 10 22

Altitude: 1020 m. *Top:* 3018 m.	Ski areas: Murschetg, Crap Sogn Gion, Crap Masegn, Vorab Glacier, Foppa-Naraus-Cassonsgrat, Startgels-Grauberg
Language: German, Romansh	
Beds: 7,300 in Laax, 5,200 in Flims	
Population: 1,283 in Laax, 2,386 in Flims	Ski schools: Schweizer Skischule Laax, Schweizer Skischule Flims
Health: Doctors and dentists in Laax and Flims. *Hospital:* Ilanz (8 km.)	Linked resorts: Falera
	Season: December to April, summer skiing on glacier
Runs: 220 km.	
Lifts: 34	Kindergarten: *Non-ski:* from 3 years. *With ski:* from 4 years

Prices: *Lift pass*: 6 days Sfr. 198 (children Sfr. 99). *Ski school*: Group Sfr. 20 for half-day (children Sfr. 18); private Sfr. 95 for half-day.

RATINGS

Skiing Conditions: 7
Snow Conditions: 5
For Beginners: 6
For Intermediates: 7
For Advanced Skiers: 7
For Children: 6
Après-Ski: 7
Other Sports: 8
Value for Money: 7

THE RESORTS

These neighbouring resorts share a common ski area, but Flims is the older and more established of the two. Equally popular in summer and winter, it has been a tourist destination for a century. It is divided into Flims Dorf and Flims Waldhaus. Dorf is where the ski lifts begin, while Waldhaus is the smarter, more residential part, where most of the hotels are located. It is quite a long walk from Waldhaus to and from the bottom of the lifts, but there is a public bus service and most hotels run their own mini-bus shuttle services in the morning and afternoons.

Laax has been developed as a ski resort much more recently, but here again the lifts are a long walk—or more realistically a bus ride—from the hotels. Murschetg is a purpose-built satellite of Laax and is closer to the lifts.

THE SKIING

The Laax/Flims ski area is known as the White Arena. The lift system is on the whole well designed, but there is a disparity between the types of lifts. To get up to Cassonsgrat (2675 m.), for instance, you first take a very fast ultra-modern chair lift, then an ancient, slow two-man sideways chair lift and finally an efficient modern cable car. The only run down from Cassonsgrat is a steep, unpisted black which begins with a 250-m. climb up above the top lift station.

There are only a handful of other black runs in the area, but some of the reds, like the run from Nagens down to Flims Dorf through narrow gulleys in the forest, are certainly pretty taxing. Most of the runs in the White Arena suffer from the same disadvantage: they are more or less south-facing and get a lot of sunshine. Therefore, this is not a place for late-season skiing, despite the presence of a glacier. On the other hand, there are some lovely wide, open intermediate slopes offering marvellous panoramic views, particularly below La Siala (2810 m.).

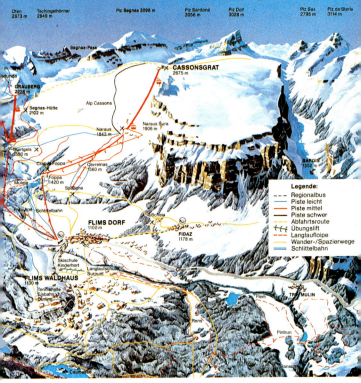

The links across to Crap Sogn Gion (2228 m.) and the Vorab glacier (3018 m.) above Laax are fairly good. The skiing over here is a mixture of easy intermediate blue runs, some fairly demanding reds and a few blacks. You have to watch the clock if you want to ski back over to Flims before the end of the day, because it is further than one imagines and the lifts close relatively early. (The glacier lifts close at 3 p.m., even in March.) Alternatively, you can ski down the black World Cup downhill course to Laax and take the bus back to Flims.

APRÈS-SKI

Flims Waldhaus has several grand old hotels, the smartest being the much-redeveloped Park Hotel Waldhaus. The clientele in Flims Waldhaus is relatively middle-aged and seems mostly satisfied with the entertainments laid on in hotel bars and nightclubs. Down in Flims Dorf, young people congregate mainly in the Albana pub, just beside the bottom of the lift station. Most of the English-speaking visitors in this area are American and many of them stay in Laax at an improbably named hotel/entertainment complex called the Happy Rancho.

OTHER ACTIVITIES

Between Laax and Flims you have 60 km. of cross-country tracks (3 km. floodlit) and 50 km. of paths for walking; skating and curling, indoor or outdoor; tobogganing, swimming, tennis, squash, horse riding, skibob and bowling.

GRÄCHEN

Access: *Nearest airport*: Geneva (2 hrs.); Zurich (3½ hrs.). *By road*: N9 motorway, exit Riddes, direction Visp, St. Niklaus. *By rail*: to Brig, then by bus.
Tourist Office: CH-3925 Grächen. Tel. (028) 56 13 00

Altitude: 1617 m. *Top:* 2870 m.	Ski areas: Wannehorn-Hannigalp, Seetalhorn-Plattja
Language: German	
Beds: 5,000	Ski schools: Schweizer Skischule Grächen
Population: 1,250	Linked resorts: None
Health: Doctor in resort. *Hospital:* Visp (25 km.)	Season: Mid-December to mid-April
Runs: 40 km.	Kindergarten: *Non-ski*: 2–6 years. *With ski*: 3–6 years.
Lifts: 14	

Prices: *Lift pass*: 6 days Sfr. 148 (children Sfr. 74). *Ski school*: Group Sfr. 18 for half-day (children Sfr. 17); private Sfr. 30 for 50 min.

RATINGS

Skiing Conditions	Snow Conditions	For Beginners	For Intermediates	For Advanced Skiers	For Children	Après-Ski	Other Sports	Value for Money
6	6	4	7	6	5	5	5	7

THE RESORT

Existing in the shadow of two much more famous resorts—Zermatt and Saas-Fee—Grächen is often ignored by skiers, particularly British ones. This is a pity, because Grächen is in fact a pretty, old-fashioned mountain village giving access to an admittedly limited but fairly taxing ski area. Most visitors to Grächen are self-catering, but the resort does boast one four-star hotel and several good three-star establishments.

THE SKIING

There is quite a bit of challenging skiing in the Grächen region, but unfortunately links between the ski areas are not good. Furthermore, there is only one run—a red—back to the resort.

This means that Grächen has limited appeal for skiers of early-intermediate standard and below, unless they are prepared to take lifts back down to the village.

Broadly speaking, the two main areas are Seetalhorn-Plattja and Wannehorn-Hannigalp. Seetalhorn is the highest (2870 m.) and most difficult part of the area, although it does also offer intermediate runs. A particularly testing descent is Bergji; the snag is that the only way out is back up by drag lift. There are several short black runs beside the Wannehorn drag lift.

The Hannigalp area, which rises up to 2114 m. is the most popular. There is a good selection of red and blue runs served by drag lifts around here. Much of the skiing is through woodland. The one red run down to the resort itself is mostly through woodland, but its mainly south-facing aspect can make it tricky to ski later in the season when it gets a lot of sun and can be icy, slushy or just bare, according to weather conditions. There is some good off-piste skiing accessible from the Grächen ski area for those in the company of a local guide.

APRÈS-SKI

Because Grächen attracts mainly family visitors, the après-ski scene is not remarkable. What little activity there is tends to take place in hotels. The Grächerhof and Walliserhof both have discos, sometimes live bands as well. The bar of the Hannigalp & Valaisia Hotel is a popular meeting-place. There are around 35 restaurants in Grächen, ranging from pizzerias to luxury establishments. The Bellevue and Romantica hotels and the Grächerhof & Schönegg Hotel are known for their good restaurants.

OTHER ACTIVITIES

On offer are 16 km. of cross-country trails, 20 km. of walks, skating, curling, indoor tennis, swimming, tobogganing, table tennis and a fitness centre. Day trips are possible to neighbouring resorts like Zermatt and Saas-Fee, although separate lift passes need to be purchased.

GRINDELWALD

Access: *Nearest airport*: Zurich (3 hrs.). *By road*: N6 motorway, exit Spiez, then via Interlaken. *By rail*: to Interlaken, then narrow-gauge railway to Grindelwald.

Tourist Office: CH-3818 Grindelwald. Tel. (036) 53 12 12

Altitude: 1050 m. *Top:* 2320 m.	Ski areas: First-Oberjoch, Kleine Scheidegg-Männlichen
Language: German	
Beds: 9,000	Ski schools: Schweizer Skischule Grindelwald
Population: 3,600	
Health: Doctors in resort. *Hospital:* Interlaken (18 km.)	Linked resorts: Wengen
	Season: Mid-December to mid-April
Runs: 41 km. (165 km. in Jungfrau Region)	Kindergarten: *Non-ski*: from 3 years. *With ski*: from 3 years.
Lifts: 28 (43 in Jungfrau Region)	

Prices: *Lift pass*: 6 days First Sfr. 128, Kleine Scheidegg-Männlichen Sfr. 160, Jungfrau Region Sfr. 188 (children Sfr. 86, 107 and 126). *Ski school*: Group Sfr. 20 for half-day; private Sfr. 38 per hour.

RATINGS

Skiing Conditions 7 / Snow Conditions 4 / For Beginners 6 / For Intermediates 8 / For Advanced Skiers 7 / For Children 6 / Après-Ski 7 / Other Sports 8 / Value for Money 7

For map see pp. 158–159.

THE RESORT

Compared to Mürren and Wengen, its partners in the Jungfrau ski region, Grindelwald is positively sophisticated. For one thing it allows cars, although this is a mixed blessing, as easy road access means a lot of weekend visitors. It has a good range of grand hotels and smart shops. Keen skiers should note that the resort is lower than Wengen or Mürren, so conditions for early- or late-season skiing are unreliable.

THE SKIING

The Grindelwald/First ski area, which rises up to 2468 m. at the Oberjoch, is ideal for intermediates and offers lots of pleasant cruising. Queues can be a problem here in high season, but new lifts are being planned to replace the existing chair lift. There are also good off-piste possibilities in this area, if you have a guide to show them to you.

For better skiers, the Kleine Scheidegg/Männlichen area is the place to head for, with its connections to Wengen and the Lauberhorn World Cup course. This is most easily reached from Grindelwald Grund, so keen skiers are well advised to stay here or else close to the station in Grindelwald.

From the top of the 25-minute-long Männlichen télécabine (for which there are often bad queues, especially at weekends) you can either ski all the way back down to Grindelwald, or use the longish chair and drag lifts on the top half of the mountain, perhaps working your way across to Kleine Scheidegg via Arvengarten. These lifts offer access to varied piste skiing, as well as some interesting off-piste.

An alternative route to Kleine Scheidegg is by train, although there can be bad queues for this too at peak periods. From Kleine Scheidegg the choices are between skiing directly back down to Grindelwald via easy runs (the last part along woodland paths), skiing the chair and drag lifts on the Männlichen side, or skiing down to Wengen via Wixi.

Grindelwald affords superb mountain views—the Wetterhorn is just one of the imposing peaks.

APRÈS-SKI

Grindelwald is reasonably lively after dark, with several small bars and cafés, although much of the nocturnal activity takes place in the main hotels. The Grand Hotel Regina is a smart, fairly formal hotel, but it has a good restaurant. Other good nightspots include the Spider at the Hotel Spinne and the Cava-Bar at Hotel Derby Bahnhof.

OTHER ACTIVITIES

Grindelwald has a vast modern sports centre which also houses the tourist office. There is a large indoor ice rink offering skating and curling, swimming and fitness. Horse riding, hang-gliding and skibob and 32 km. of cross-country trails are also available.

There is a spectacular excursion (not included on the lift pass) from Kleine Scheidegg by train up through the inside of the Jungfrau mountain to the Jungfraujoch, which at 3454 m. is the highest railway station in Europe.

GSTAAD

Access: *Nearest airport*: Geneva (2½ hrs.) *By road*: N12 motorway, exit Bulle, then direction Saanen. *By rail*: express to Aigle or Bulle, then connection to Gstaad, or MOB railway from Montreux.
Tourist Office: CH-3780 Gstaad. Tel. (030) 4 10 55

Altitude: 1100 m. *Top:* 3000 m.	Ski areas: Eggli, Wispile, Wasserngrat
Language: German	
Beds: 1,000 in hotels, 2,500 in chalets and apartments	Ski schools: Schweizer Skischule Gstaad
Population: 2,000	Linked resorts: Rougemont, Saanen, Schönried, Saanenmöser, Gsteig, St. Stephan, Lauenen, Zweisimmen
Health: Doctors and hospital in resort.	
Runs: 250 km. in Gstaad Superski Region	Season: December to April
Lifts: 14 (69 in Gstaad Superski Region)	Kindergarten: *Non-ski*: 4–8 years. *With ski*: none, but ski school from 4 years.

Prices: *Lift pass*: 6 days Sfr. 188 (children Sfr. 113). *Ski school*: Group Sfr. 19 for half-day; private Sfr. 40 per hour.

RATINGS — Skiing Conditions: 6 / Snow Conditions: 5 / For Beginners: 6 / For Intermediates: 7 / For Advanced Skiers: 7 / For Children: 5 / Après-Ski: 7 / Other Sports: 7 / Value for Money: 7

THE RESORT

Despite its jet-set clientele and reputation, Gstaad remains a pretty Alpine village. You are as likely to see a farmer driving a tractor pulling a cartload of manure through the main street as you are to see a fur-clad film star driving a Rolls Royce. The jet-set season, which is largely focused on the Palace Hotel, is short—January and February—and outside of these times Gstaad can really be very quiet. It is far smaller and less pretentious than St. Moritz, with which it is so often linked by gossip columnists.

THE SKIING

Gstaad is part of a ski area formerly known as the Weisse Hochland, the White Highlands, now being renamed the Gstaad Superski Region. It comprises ten resorts which are on the same lift pass and are as much as 30 km. apart—they include Saanenmöser, Schönried and Zweisimmen. For this reason, it is a good area for exploring if you have a car at your disposal.

There are three main ski areas which begin in Gstaad itself, but they all have different starting points. The Eggli system has some

good long intermediate runs and connects with the neighbouring village of Rougemont. From here you can either take a télécabine back up and ski down to Eggli or take a train (included in the lift pass) back to Gstaad.

The Wasserngrat is probably the most famous mountain in Gstaad: close to its peak is the Eagle Club—the most exclusive lunch club in the Alps. (Those without membership must be content to dine in the nearby Wasserngrat restaurant, which does excellent *rösti.*) There is a wide range of runs down from here—something to please intermediates and experts alike. With a guide you can find good off-piste runs through the trees, especially in powder-snow conditions. The Wispile area is rather less challenging, but there are still quite a few runs that will interest the advanced intermediate.

APRÈS-SKI

For the fashionable, après-ski centres on the Palace Hotel—its Grill, Fromagerie and Sans Cravatte are all popular, as is the Greengo disco/nightclub. More relaxed entertainment can be found in the charming Hotel Olden, right in the centre of town.

This is a popular rendezvous spot immediately after skiing, and the hotel's La Cave restaurant has a good reputation. For a cheap dinner you can have a pizza at the Arc-en-Ciel, or spend slightly more and go to the Posthotel Rössli for Swiss specialities. A little out of town, the Chlösterli, a converted monastery, is fun if you are with a group.

The cinema shows films in various languages, including English, and exhibitions are organized round the local craftwork of paper-cuts.

OTHER ACTIVITIES

Non-skiers will not feel alone in Gstaad; many visitors come simply to relax, promenade and party. There are 50 km. of walks and 30 km. of cross-country tracks in the vicinity. Other sports include swimming, skating (artificial and natural rinks), curling, horse riding, tennis, squash, tobogganing and hot-air ballooning.

HAUTE-NENDAZ

Access: *Nearest airport*: Geneva (2½ hrs.). *By road*: N9 motorway, exit Riddes, then via Sion. *By rail*: to Sion, then post bus.
Tourist Office: CH-1961 Haute-Nendaz. Tel. (027) 88 14 44

Altitude: 1320 m. *Top:* 3328 m.

Language: French

Beds: 15,000

Population: 1,500

Health: Doctor in resort. *Hospital:* Sion (15 km.)

Runs: 120 km. (320 km. in 4 Vallées area)

Lifts: 32 (86 in 4 Vallées area)

Ski areas: Tracouet, Prarion, Plan de Fou

Ski schools: Ecole Suisse de Ski Nendaz

Linked resorts: Verbier, Mayens-de-Riddes, Veysonnaz, Thyon 2000, Les Collons

Season: Mid-December to mid-April; summer skiing on glacier

Kindergarten: *Non-ski:* 3–5 years. *With ski:* 3–5 years.

Prices: *Lift pass*: 6 days Sfr. 184 (children Sfr. 94). *Ski school*: Group Sfr. 19 for half-day; private Sfr. 40 per hour.

RATINGS

Skiing Conditions	Snow Conditions	For Beginners	For Intermediates	For Advanced Skiers	For Children	Après-Ski	Other Sports	Value for Money
7	7	7	7	7	7	6	6	7

For map see pp. 142–143.

THE RESORT

Haute-Nendaz and its small satellite of Super-Nendaz (Siviez) are essentially modern resorts, consisting mainly of architecturally unremarkable chalet-style apartment blocks. Haute-Nendaz lacks both the sophistication and the pretty aspect of Verbier, but its aficionados argue that its great advantage is much easier access to the Tortin/Mont-Fort skiing.

Access to Haute-Nendaz is by a tortuous road up from Sion in the Rhône valley, significantly further away from Geneva than Verbier, which is reached by a much easier road up from the more westerly valley town of Martigny.

THE SKIING

The ski area available to those based in Haute-Nendaz is essentially that normally ascribed to Verbier. However, since the opening of the new 150-person "Le Jumbo" cable car from La Chaux to Col des Gentianes, which has greatly improved access to Mont-Fort for Verbier-based skiers, Haute-Nendaz's claim to provide quicker access to this region looks less impressive. In any case, skiers based in Haute-Nendaz normally have to take a bus to Super-Nendaz and then risk queues before taking three lifts, the last of them a drag lift along the flat, to the bottom of Tortin.

From Tortin, you can either take the bubble up to the top of the notorious mogul-ridden Tortin run itself, or take the cable car up to Col des Gentianes. From here you can take a further cable car up to the very top of Mont-Fort (3328 m.), ski down a long run to Verbier's La Chaux, returning in "Le Jumbo" unless you wish to explore more of Verbier's ski area, or take a longish taxing run from Col des Gentianes back to the bottom of Tortin. Note that it is necessary to pay the Mont-Fort supplement to the standard 4 Vallées lift pass in order to ski in this area. This supplement is best bought on a daily basis since weather is uncertain; storms and avalanche danger can often close the Mont-Fort sector. No supplement is levied for using the Tortin télécabine, which gives access to Verbier's Lac des Vaux, Les Attelas and other ski areas.

The skiing immediately above Haute-Nendaz itself is mainly

intermediate, but the relative steepness of some of the slopes makes them unsuitable for early intermediates or near-beginners. Queues can sometimes be a problem at peak times on the lifts that converge at Tracouet. The piste under the Plan-du-Fou cable car makes it possible to ski down to Super-Nendaz, although this run is sometimes closed due to avalanche danger. Taking the bus will usually be quicker anyway.

APRÈS-SKI

Haute-Nendaz is principally a resort dedicated to families and other groups who come on self-catering holidays, so the après-ski scene is not really sophisticated. However, the resort is by no means dead at night. Principal après-ski venues include Les Flambeaux, which offers everything from pizzas and crêpes to dancing; Le Lapin Vert, a disco catering mainly for the French-speaking market; and Le Tchin Tchin, a piano bar.

OTHER ACTIVITIES

Some 56 km. of cross-country trails link up with Siviez and there are 20 km. of walking paths, as well as skating, curling, swimming (at Siviez), tobogganing, squash and fitness. Trips down to valley towns such as Sion are possible.

KLOSTERS

Access: *Nearest airport*: Zurich (2 hrs.). *By road*: N3 motorway, exit Landquart. *By rail*: to Landquart, then Rhaetian railway to Klosters.

Tourist Office: CH-7250 Klosters. Tel. (083) 4 18 77

Altitude: 1200 m. *Top*: 2844 m.

Language: German

Beds: 2,000 in hotels and 6,600 in apartments

Population: 3,500

Health: Doctors and dentist in resort. *Hospital:* Davos (10 km.)

Runs: 152 (320 km. with Davos)

Lifts: 26 (55 with Davos)

Ski areas: Madrisa, Gotschna-Parsenn

Ski schools: Schweizer Ski-schule Klosters

Linked resorts: Davos

Season: December to April

Kindergarten: *Non-ski*: 2–5 years. *With ski*: none, but ski school from 4 years.

Prices: *Lift pass*: 6 days Madrisa Sfr. 140 (children Sfr. 105). *Ski school*: Group Sfr. 22 for half-day (children Sfr. 20); private Sfr. 40 for 50 min.

RATINGS

Skiing Conditions	Snow Conditions	For Beginners	For Intermediates	For Advanced Skiers	For Children	Après-Ski	Other Sports	Value for Money
8	6	6	7	8	6	7	7	7

Madrisa

Madrisa 2826 m
Schafflurggli 2394 m
Zügenhüttli
Saaser Alp 1900 m
Dorf 1124 m
Klosters
Kubis 814 m
Landjurt
Saas 938 m
Selfrangg 990 m
Platz 1200 m
Selfrangg Bad
Doggilochtr.
Selfranga
Gotschnaboden 1787 m

Prättigau

Gotschna / Parsenn

Weissfluhgipfel 2844 m
Weissfluhjoch 2663 m
Parsenn-furka 2435 m
Casanna 2557 m
Contersor Schwend
Gotschnagrat 2300 m
Parsennhütte 2205 m
Davos

THE RESORT

In contrast to the neighbouring town of Davos, with which it shares a skiing area, Klosters is a small, traditional Alpine village which has been relatively unsullied by mass tourism. Socially, it is a very smart resort, well patronized by aristocrats and royals, particularly British ones. Klosters comprises mainly chalets, in which much of the classiest socializing goes on, but there are also several smart hotels and apartment blocks.

THE SKIING

The principal ski area for Klosters is the Gotschna sector which leads over towards Davos and connects with the Parsenn area and in turn with the Weissfluhjoch and the Schatzalp/Strela areas. There are plenty of wide, cruising pistes in the Parsenn area, but skiers in search of more difficult terrain should proceed to the top of the Weissfluhgipfel and try the runs down beside the Parsennbahn to Davos, or alternatively ski the Gipfel Nord run towards Kreuzweg. For a real challenge, skiers can try the Wang run which is directly under the Gotschna cable car. It has a reputation for being one of the most difficult runs in Europe, but it is often closed due to lack of snow or danger of avalanche.

There is some pleasant, picturesque skiing through forests down to valley villages like Conters and Serneus, from where you can catch a train back to Klosters. These forest trails also take you to the charming Schwendi houses—rustic mountain restaurants specializing in all kinds of *rösti*.

The Madrisa sector on the other side of the Klosters valley rises up to 2542 m. and offers pleasant, undemanding skiing. There are about half a dozen drag lifts up here, but the area is really of interest only to early-intermediates and sun-worshippers.

APRÈS-SKI

Much of the smartest après-ski in Klosters takes place behind closed doors in private chalets, but there is still plenty of stylish activity in the resort's hotels, particularly the Chesa Grischuna. The Cellar Bar here is a popular rendezvous point. The greatest

KLOSTERS

dinner to be had in Klosters is at the Hotel Wynegg, where the speciality is *fondue chinoise* (meat fondue cooked in bouillon, with various sauces). This unpretentious hotel is where Prince Charles used to stay in his bachelor days. Later at night, the Casa Antica is the best disco.

OTHER ACTIVITIES

There are 40 km. of cross-country trails, plus skating (on a natural rink), curling, swimming (in hotels), squash, fitness centre, 34 km. of cleared walks, tobogganing and sleigh-rides. For a breath of culture, there are three art galleries, and the local history museum opens three times a week. A wider range of activities is available in neighbouring Davos.

LENK

Access: *Nearest airport*: Geneva (3 hrs.); Zurich (2 hrs.). *By road*: N6 motorway, exit Wimmis, then via Zweisimmen. *By rail:* to Montreux, then Montreux-Bernese-Oberland (MOB) railway.
Tourist Office: CH-3775 Lenk. Tel. (030) 3 15 95

Altitude: 1068 m. *Top:* 2099 m.

Language: German

Beds: 6,200

Population: 2,400

Health: Doctors and spa centre in resort.
Hospital: Zweisimmen (13 km.)

Runs: 120 km. (240 km. with Adelboden)

Lifts: 20 (50 with Adelboden)

Ski areas: Betelberg-Leiterli, Bühlberg-Hahnenmoos

Ski schools: Schweizer Skischule Lenk

Linked resorts: Adelboden

Season: Mid-December to mid-April

Kindergarten: *Non-ski*: from 3 years. *With ski*: none, but ski school from 3 years.

Prices: *Lift pass*: 6 days Sfr. 157 (children Sfr. 97). *Ski school*: Group Sfr. 17 for half-day; private Sfr. 38 per hour.

RATINGS

Skiing Conditions	Snow Conditions	For Beginners	For Intermediates	For Advanced Skiers	For Children	Après-Ski	Other Sports	Value for Money
6	5	6	7	4	5	4	7	7

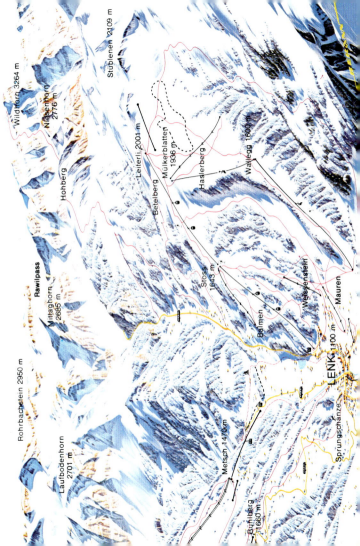

LENK

THE RESORT

Linking with Adelboden and situated in the canton of Bern, Lenk is a thermal spa village as well as a ski resort, lying at the foot of the Wildstrubel mountain. This is a quiet, restful resort, more suited to the middle-aged and families than young people. There has been quite a bit of development in Lenk over the past few years, mostly of apartment blocks. However, there is a good selection of four- and three-star hotels. Lenk has a large and loyal German clientele.

THE SKIING

Happily, the Lenk ski area is much less spread out than that of neighbouring Adelboden. It consists basically of two areas: Hahnenmoos, which links with Adelboden, and Leiterli/Betelberg, on the opposite side of the resort.

In both areas the majority of the pistes are of an intermediate standard. There is a good long run from Metschstand, on the Hahnenmoos side, back down to resort level, but even so it is doubtful whether the challenge this run offers is worth the difficulty of getting to its start: you must first take a bus, then a cable car, then two drag lifts. The other runs around Metsch are mostly broad, intermediate pistes of little interest to advanced skiers. The same is true of the run down from Hahnenmoos.

The Leiterli/Betelberg area is more easily and quickly reached from Lenk itself since the télécabine starts fairly close to the centre of the village. This is a two-stage télécabine, and from the intermediate station of Stoss (1643 m.) there is a fairly testing black run back to the bottom. From Stoss, the second stage of the télécabine rises up to Betelberg (1960 m.). Around here there are

plenty of pleasing but undemanding red and blue runs, some of them passing through woodland right down to village level and others crossing over towards the Wallegg chair lift which ascends to 1936 m., but for which there are often queues.

APRÈS-SKI

As might be expected, après-ski in Lenk is mainly sedate and geared towards the middle-aged majority of the clientele. There is a good selection of restaurants—over 30 in all—and dancing at the smartest hotel in town: the Kurhotel Lenkerhof. Both the Lenkerhof and Parkhotel Bellevue have piano bars.

OTHER ACTIVITIES

Lenk is a good place for non-skiers and those who prefer the sport in its cross-country form. There are 40 km. of cross-country tracks, 30 km. of paths for walking, as well as skating, curling, swimming, tobogganing, sleigh-rides, a spa and flights around the glacier.

LENZERHEIDE-VALBELLA

Access: *Nearest airport*: Zurich (2½ hrs.). *By road*: N13 motorway, exit Chur-Süd. *By rail*: to Chur, then by bus.
Tourist Office: CH-7078 Lenzerheide. Tel. (081) 34 34 34

Altitude: 1500 m. *Top:* 2865 m.	Ski areas: Rothorn-Scalottas, Danis, Stätzerhorn
Language: German	
Beds: 2,000 in hotels, 6,000 in apartments	Ski schools: Schweizer Skischule Lenzerheide, Schweizer Skischule Valbella, Caselva Skischule Valbella
Population: 2,500	
Health: Doctors in resort. *Hospital:* Chur (17 km.)	Linked resorts: Parpan, Churwalden
Runs: 155 km.	Season: December to April
Lifts: 37	Kindergarten: *Non-ski*: no age limit. *With ski*: from 3 years.

Prices: *Lift pass*: 6 days Sfr. 162 (children Sfr. 97). *Ski school*: Group Sfr. 20 for half-day (children Sfr. 19); private Sfr. 45 per hour.

RATINGS

Skiing Conditions	Snow Conditions	For Beginners	For Intermediates	For Advanced Skiers	For Children	Après-Ski	Other Sports	Value for Money
6	5	6	7	5	6	6	7	7

THE RESORT

Lenzerheide is the better-known resort in a complex that is nowadays called Lenzerheide-Valbella. These two villages were originally separated by the Heidsee lake, but expansion along the lakeside has meant that they now virtually sprawl into one another. Popular in summer as well as winter, both of these are long-established, traditional resorts.

Lying in the Grisons canton on the road to the Julier Pass, Lenzerheide is not as well known in Britain as the nearby larger resorts in this canton such as St. Moritz, Klosters and Davos. However, in the 60s and early 70s the place was a popular destination for English family holidays—the Thatcher family, for example, visited Lenzerheide regularly.

Lenzerheide itself is not an especially pretty resort, with grand hotels in the traditional Swiss style, but the setting is pretty and there are lovely views across the lake and through woodland to the mountains below.

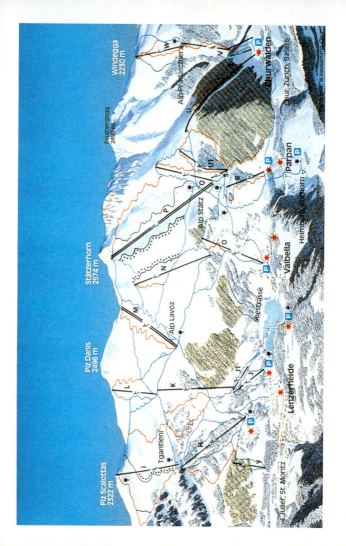

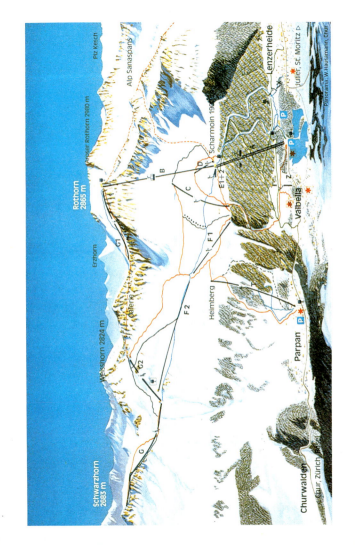

LENZERHEIDE-VALBELLA

THE SKIING

The skiing in the Lenzerheide region is divided into two separate areas which do not really interconnect. You have to come back down to the village to get from one to another—indeed you usually need to take a bus because the lifts on the Rothorn side lie an inconvenient walk from the village itself.

The Rothorn side is where the best skiing is to be found, and a two-stage cable car, for which there are often long queues, ascends from the resort level of 1500 m. to 2865 m. There are some red and black runs down from here—the most difficult in the resort. The Rothorn also gives access to some interesting off-piste runs, including some which link up with the resort of Arosa, which lies in the next valley.

The skiing on the other side of the Lenzerheide valley consists of a lot of wide, intermediate slopes and very little that is more challenging. On the other hand, there are plenty of drag lifts over here, so queues are rare. The highest point in this system is 2431 m.

There are also tricky connections to lift systems in the nearby villages of Parpan and Churwalden.

APRÈS-SKI

Lenzerheide's après-ski tends to revolve, not surprisingly, around its numerous hotels. The grandest and most important of these is the Grand Hotel Kurhaus Alpina. Its Steivetta bar is a popular meeting-place and the Tic-Tac nightclub is the only noteworthy one in the resort. Otherwise there are some quiet but pleasant cafés/restaurants around the resort. In Valbella the Posthotel Valbella and the Valbella-Inn are the principal après-ski venues.

OTHER ACTIVITIES

Bowling at the Hotel Schweizerhof is a popular après-ski activity. In addition there are 50 km. of cross-country tracks, 35 km. of prepared walks, skating, curling, swimming, squash, indoor tennis and sleigh-rides.

LEYSIN

⛷ ⛷ +

Access: *Nearest airport*: Geneva (1½ hrs.). *By road*: N9 motorway, exit Aigle. *By rail*: to Aigle, then COP railway to Leysin.
Tourist Office: CH-1854 Leysin. Tel. (025) 34 22 44

Altitude: 1200 m. *Top:* 2200 m.

Language: French

Beds: 7,000

Population: 2,000

Health: Doctors, dentist and clinic in resort.
Hospital: Aigle (15 km.)

Runs: 60 km.

Lifts: 19

Ski areas: Solacyre, Berneuse, Mayen, Le Fer

Ski schools: Ecole Suisse de Ski Leysin

Linked resorts: None

Season: Mid-December to mid-April

Kindergarten: *Non-ski*: none. *With ski*: 4–6 years.

Prices: *Lift pass*: 6 days Sfr. 130 (children Sfr. 90). *Ski school*: Group Sfr. 20 for half-day (children Sfr. 15); private Sfr. 40 per hour.

RATINGS

Skiing Conditions	Snow Conditions	For Beginners	For Intermediates	For Advanced Skiers	For Children	Après-Ski	Other Sports	Value for Money
6	5	7	7	4	6	7	7	7

THE RESORT

Like quite a few of the older, more traditional Swiss Alpine resorts, Leysin first came into existence as a health resort. The many sanatoria here were used mainly for the treatment of tuberculosis, back in the days when mountain air and sunshine were thought beneficial for the condition. In more recent times it has become a popular location for international schools and colleges, and the students at these establishments certainly help to give the resort a young, lively international air.

The village is not especially pretty to look at, consisting as it does of a variety of rather institutional-looking hotels and other buildings of disparate architectural styles. However, Leysin does have a beautifully sunny position, lying up above the Rhône valley town of Aigle, in the canton of Vaud. It is reached either by road or by mountain railway running up from Aigle, with several stops in the resort.

THE SKIING

Although Leysin has expanded its ski area significantly over the past few years, it remains a resort for advanced intermediates and below, rather than for experts, and the lift system does not link together completely.

The main access routes into the ski area are the télécabines to Berneuse and Mayen, both of which run from the same lift station in the resort. These lifts are subject to very long queues in high season, particularly around the morning peak period. Another problem is that they are often out of action due to high winds, making access to further lifts difficult. Construction of new drag lifts, however, is helping to ameliorate this situation.

On the Mayen sector, the pistes are all easy, pretty and sun-soaked. The runs back to the resort through some woodland, although not difficult, are good fun. At the top of the Berneuse télécabine (2048 m.) there is a spectacular Alpine panorama and a revolving restaurant for lunching skiers to appreciate it at their leisure. The runs down from Berneuse are not generally all that exciting: in any case many of them eventually merge with those from Mayen. Leysin's only black run starts a short way from the top station and quickly leads you into a taxing mogul field.

Adventurous skiers, especially those who have the use of a car, may well choose to use Leysin as a base from which to make day trips to some of the neighbouring resorts: Villars and Les Diablerets are the most obvious destinations, but places like Gstaad and Château-d'Œx are also within reach, as indeed is Verbier. All these resorts, however, do require separate lift passes.

APRÈS-SKI

Leysin offers a good variety of nightlife to suit students and young visitors, as well as its more sedate guests. The aptly named Club Vagabond is the place where most of the young "in crowd" can be found dancing and drinking. Other discos include the Grenier and the Casanova, but there is also a selection of bars and piano

bars. The best restaurant in Leysin is probably Le Feydey, which is known for its fish dishes. Le Leysin is a cheaper alternative with plenty of atmosphere but reasonable prices.

OTHER ACTIVITIES

Leysin boasts 15 km. of cross-country trails, 30 km. of walks, skating, curling, swimming, indoor tennis and squash, horse riding, para-gliding, sleigh-rides and a fitness centre. Excursions to Montreux, Vevey and Lausanne on Lake Geneva are possible by train, changing at Aigle.

MORGINS

Access: *Nearest airport*: Geneva (2 hrs.). *By road*: N9 motorway, exit Aigle, then direction Monthey. *By rail*: to Aigle, then AOMC railway to Troistorrents and post bus.

Tourist Office: CH-1875 Morgins. Tel. (025) 77 23 61

Altitude: 1400 m. *Top:* 2000 m.	Ski areas: La Foilleuse, Le Corbeau
Language: French	
Beds: 6,000	Ski schools: Ecole Suisse de Ski Morgins
Population: 380	
Health: Doctor in Troistorrents (7 km.). *Hospital:* Monthey (13 km.)	Linked resorts: Portes du Soleil resorts
	Season: Mid-December to mid-April
Runs: 650 km. in Portes du Soleil area	Kindergarten: *Non-ski*: from 3 years. *With ski*: none, but ski school from 4 years.
Lifts: 16 (220 in Portes du Soleil area)	

Prices: *Lift pass*: 6 days Sfr. 170 (children Sfr. 119). *Ski school*: Group Sfr. 18 for half-day; private Sfr. 38 per hour.

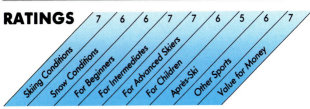

RATINGS: Skiing Conditions 7 / Snow Conditions 6 / For Beginners 6 / For Intermediates 7 / For Advanced Skiers 7 / For Children 6 / Après-Ski 5 / Other Sports 6 / Value for Money 7

For map see pp. 40–41.

THE RESORT

After Champéry, Morgins is the second most important Swiss resort in the vast Portes du Soleil ski network. Like Champéry it is an old-fashioned Alpine village in which farming is given equal priority to skiing. Smaller than Champéry, it is very close to Châtel in France.

As a base from which to ski the Portes du Soleil area, it has the advantage of being 1400 m. high—350 m. higher than Champéry, so snow is rather more reliable at either end of the season. There are many pretty old chalets in Morgins, and most of the newer buildings have been built in chalet style.

THE SKIING

Morgins is not close to the most challenging skiing in the Portes du Soleil area, but it does provide easy access to some of the region's pleasantest skiing. These runs are mostly in the direction of Châtel and are often through woodland, unlike most in this complex.

On the other side of Morgins, the lifts connect with the neighbouring Swiss resort of Champoussin which is an impressive 1680 m. high. Many of these runs are also through woodland, and there is a good assortment of drag lifts for early intermediates to practise on, including one excellent intermediate trail through pine trees to the village. Around the village of Morgins itself there are pleasant, sunny nursery slopes.

Morgins is even closer to Geneva, Lausanne and other population centres than Châtel, so it too is prone to overcrowding problems caused by day-trippers at weekends and at holiday times.

APRÈS-SKI

Morgins is a small, charming, slightly sleepy resort and its après-ski is not its biggest attraction. Nevertheless, the Hostellerie Bellevue, the resort's main hotel (modern, but chalet-style) has quite a bit to offer, including a bar, several restaurants and a disco/nightclub. Otherwise there are a few unpretentious bars and restaurants.

OTHER ACTIVITIES

There are 20 km. of cross-country tracks, skating and curling (natural rink), swimming (in the Hostellerie Bellevue) and indoor tennis. Morgins is well placed for excursions down to Lake Geneva and the towns on its banks: Montreux, Lausanne, Geneva on the Swiss side, and Evian and Thonon on the French side.

MÜRREN

Access: *Nearest airport*: Zurich (3 hrs.). *By road*: to Lauterbrunnen, then train, or to Stechelberg, then cable car. *By rail*: to Interlaken, then BOB/BLM railway.
Tourist Office: CH-3825 Mürren. Tel. (036) 55 16 16

Altitude: 1650 m. *Top:* 2970 m.	Ski areas: Schilthorn, Winteregg
Language: German	
Beds: 800 in hotels, 1,200 in chalets	Ski schools: Schweizer Skischule Mürren
Population: 336	Linked resorts: None
Health: Doctor in resort. *Hospital:* Interlaken (12 km.)	Season: Mid-December to mid-April
Runs: 50 km.	Kindergarten: *Non-ski:* from 4 months. *With ski:* from 3 years.
Lifts: 8	

Prices: *Lift pass*: 6 days Sfr. 148 (children Sfr. 99). *Ski school*: Group Sfr. 19 for half-day; private Sfr. 90 for half-day.

RATINGS

Skiing Conditions	Snow Conditions	For Beginners	For Intermediates	For Advanced Skiers	For Children	Après-Ski	Other Sports	Value for Money
6	7	6	6	7	6	5	7	7

THE RESORT

Mürren is a tiny Alpine village with a permanent population of just over 300 and only 2,000 guest beds. It is a pretty, car-free place reached by a combination of funicular and train from Lauterbrunnen. It is the home of the famous Kandahar Ski Club, and many British visitors have been coming here regularly every year for generations.

THE SKIING

For such a small place, Mürren does offer some remarkably good skiing. The most famous summit here is the Schilthorn (2970 m.), where there is the Piz Gloria revolving restaurant. (This was used as the location for a James Bond film over 20 years ago, but the restaurant still makes much of this association.) The top section of the run down from the Schilthorn is very difficult, with large icy moguls covering a steep narrow path. After this, the run widens out for a few hundred yards before it becomes a long *schuss* along a path.

There are several apparently unremarkable T-bar drag lifts in Mürren which actually give access to some fairly demanding black runs. The Gimmeln lift, for instance, offers two good short blacks known as the Kandahar and the Black Line.

The Allmendhubel and Winteregg sections of the Mürren ski area offer intermediate skiing, much of it through wooded areas.

Mürren comes alive at the end of January each year for the Inferno downhill race, which has been run since 1928 and is organized by the Kandahar and Mürren ski clubs. The course runs from the top of the Schilthorn right down to Lauterbrunnen, if snow conditions permit. Only around 1,500 people can participate, whereas more than 4,000 request start numbers.

APRÈS-SKI

There is not much après-ski life here and what there is tends to revolve around hotels. The Eiger and the Jungfrau both have good bars and restaurants, and the Eiger has a nightclub, often with live music.

OTHER ACTIVITIES

Mürren has a remarkably large and modern sports centre for a resort of its size. Facilities include swimming, skating (artificial outdoor ice rink), curling, squash and tennis. There is a 1½-km. cross-country track in Mürren and a 12-km. track down in the Lauterbrunnen valley, 15 km. of walks, sleigh-rides and a toboggan run to Gimmelwald.

Day trips to Wengen and perhaps on up to Kleine Scheidegg are included on the Jungfrau Region pass. The trip up from Kleine Scheidegg through the Jungfrau is extra but spectacular.

PONTRESINA

Access: *Nearest airport*: Zurich (3½ hrs.) *By road*: N13 motorway, exit Chur, then via Lenzerheide and Julier-Pass. *By rail*: to Chur, then connection to Pontresina.

Tourist Office: CH-7504 Pontresina. Tel. (082) 6 64 88

Altitude: 1800 m. *Top:* 3304 m.

Language: German, Romansh

Beds: 5,970

Population: 1,730

Health: Doctors and dentist in resort.
Hospital: Samedan (5 km.)

Runs: 350 km. in Oberengadin

Lifts: 12 (61 in Oberengadin)

Ski areas: Diavolezza, Piz Lagalb, Bernina, Muottas Muragl, Alp Languard

Ski schools: Schweizer Skischule Pontresina

Linked resorts: None

Season: Beginning December to end April; summer skiing on glacier

Kindergarten: *Non-ski*: 3–7 years. *With ski*: 3–12 years.

Prices: *Lift pass*: 6 days Sfr. 190 (children Sfr. 140). *Ski school*: Group Sfr. 35 per day; private Sfr. 50 per hour.

RATINGS

Skiing Conditions	Snow Conditions	For Beginners	For Intermediates	For Advanced Skiers	For Children	Après-Ski	Other Sports	Value for Money
6	5	6	6	5	6	7	7	7

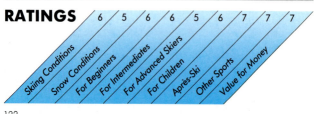

THE RESORT

Originally a summer resort, Pontresina, which lies at the beginning of the Bernina Pass from the Engadine over into Italy, has a reputation for being the "poor man's St. Moritz". This description is both fair and unfair; Pontresina is a resort in its own right and has its own character, but at the same time it is a useful base for those who want to sample the St. Moritz area without paying St. Moritz prices.

Surrounded by woodland, Pontresina is well sheltered from the worst of the elements and has great views towards the mountains. It also still has many buildings in the old Engadine style, not many of which can be seen in St. Moritz.

THE SKIING

Although there is public transport around the Engadine area, it is not always convenient for skiers. To get the most out of the region you really need to have a car at your disposal. This is particularly true of Pontresina, which does not really have any skiing of its own. Most of the driving necessary is along the floor of the valley, so roads are normally in good condition.

Pontresina is in fact closer to the challenging ski areas of Diavolezza and Piz Lagalb, which lie towards the Bernina Pass, than St. Moritz. Both of these areas offer appealing longish runs for good intermediates and above. Off the back of Diavolezza there is a famous, and famously challenging, off-piste run.

The two main St. Moritz ski areas are Corviglia and Corvatsch. Corviglia is directly above the resort itself, although it can also be reached by lift from St. Moritz Bad on the valley floor. The runs here are mostly intermediate, although there are a few more-taxing descents. Corvatsch offers a greater variety of difficult runs down from its glacier peak of 3304 m., where there is also some summer skiing.

For a superb mountain lunch, go to La Marmite at the top of the Corviglia railway and expect to pay a lot. For a more modest meal, with fantastic views and the opportunity to do a bit of intermediate skiing, drive to Muottas Muragl, which is on the way to Celerina.

APRÈS-SKI

Those looking for sophisticated nightlife will naturally have to head over to St. Moritz, but those happy with informal après-ski, based mainly around hotels, will be content with Pontresina. The Sarazena is a smart restaurant-cum-nightclub in a converted Engadine house. Most of the larger hotels stage some sort of entertainment of their own. The cinema sometimes shows films in English.

OTHER ACTIVITIES

Being on the valley floor, Pontresina is well placed for those who want to take advantage of the 150 km. of cross-country trails in the Engadine area. There are almost as many kilometres of paths for walkers in the region. For less energetic excursions, you can take the Bernina Express railway into Italy or the Glacier Express over to Zermatt. Additional activities include skating, curling, tobogganing and swimming, horse riding and sleigh-rides. The Alpine Museum is open from Monday to Saturday, and you can visit the exquisite little Chapel of Santa Maria, famed for its 13th–15th-century frescoes and the adjacent pentagonal Moorish tower.

ROUGEMONT

Access: *Nearest airport*: Geneva (2½ hrs.). *By road*: N12 motorway, exit Bulle, direction Montbovon, Château-d'Œx. *By rail*: to Montreux, then Montreux-Bernese-Oberland (MOB) railway.
Tourist Office: CH-1838 Rougemont. Tel. (029) 4 83 33

Altitude: 1000 m. *Top:* 2186 m.	Lifts: 2 m (69 in Gstaad Superski Region)
Language: French	
Beds: 180 in hotels, 350 in chalets, apartments and private homes	Ski areas: Videmanette, Chalberhöni
	Ski schools: Ecole Suisse de Ski Rougemont
Population: 895	Linked resorts: Saanen, Gstaad
Health: Doctor in resort. *Hospital:* Saanen (4 km.) or Château-d'Œx (7 km.)	Season: Mid-December to mid-April
Runs: 50 km. (250 km. in Gstaad Superski Region)	Kindergarten: *Non-ski*: none. *With ski*: 4–14 years.

Prices: *Lift pass*: 6 days Sfr. 180. *Ski school*: Group Sfr. 16 for half-day; private Sfr. 38 per hour.

RATINGS

Skiing Conditions	Snow Conditions	For Beginners	For Intermediates	For Advanced Skiers	For Children	Après-Ski	Other Sports	Value for Money
5	4	6	6	5	5	5	6	7

For map see pp. 90–91.

THE RESORT

Rougemont is a pretty, traditional Alpine village in the Vaud canton, situated between Gstaad and Château-d'Œx. It forms part of the White Highlands ski area, now officially known as the Gstaad Superski Region. This is an ideal place for those who want to holiday in an old-fashioned mountain village rather than a modern ski resort. The disadvantages of Rougemont are that the resort itself is fairly low—1000 m.—which means unreliable snow at either end of the season, and that the main ski area is a bit of a trek from the centre of the village.

THE SKIING

Like with other resorts in the White Highlands ski area, your stay in Rougemont is enhanced if you have the use of a car. Although it is possible to travel by public transport—often train—between the different resorts covered by the lift pass, it is really much easier to have your own private means of transport available. Places like Gstaad with its three areas—Wasserngrat, Eggli and Wispile—are within easy reach, as indeed are Schönried, Saanenmöser and Château-d'Œx. (Gstaad's Eggli area does in fact link with Rougemont by ski.)

However, Rougemont is fortunate in being able to offer some of the most challenging skiing in the White Highlands area. This is to be found on the Videmanette mountain which rises to 2186 m. and is reached via a two-stage télécabine from the bottom station outside the village of Rougemont. There is a very tricky, steep and narrow off-piste run down the front of Videmanette, but it is often closed—definitely for experts only. The runs from the back of Videmanette are varied, but those wishing to avoid the initial steep mogul-ridden slopes can take a short télécabine downhill. From the bottom of this télécabine (one of the strangest lifts in the Alps) there is some pleasing wide, open skiing leading to a chair lift. The run back down to the resort continues past the bottom of this chair lift and affords good intermediate skiing, great views and some intriguing paths on its way back to the valley floor. There are also alternative runs back to the resort from the middle station of the main two-stage télécabine.

APRÈS-SKI

Rougemont is essentially quiet after dark, as one would expect of such a small village. But what little activity there is tends to be of a high calibre. The Cerf restaurant serves excellent fondues and other cheese dishes and has a good, rustic atmosphere. The prices are very reasonable despite it being a popular place with celebrities from Gstaad. The Buffet de la Gare in the Hôtel Valrose and the Hôtel du Commune are also popular eating places. Those searching for sophisticated nightlife and discos must head out of Rougemont to neighbouring Gstaad.

OTHER ACTIVITIES

Apart from 35 km. of cross-country trails and 10 km. of paths for walkers, there are no other organized sporting activities. You can visit the beautiful 11th-century church, built by the Cluny monks, and the Museum of Minerals and Fossils is open twice a week.

SAAS-FEE

Access: *Nearest airport*: Geneva (3½ hrs.). *By road*: N9 motorway, exit Sion, then via Visp and Stalden. *By rail*: to Visp or Brig, then post bus.
Tourist Office: CH-3906 Saas-Fee. Tel. (028) 57 14 57

Altitude: 1800 m. *Top*: 3500 m.	Ski areas: Felskinn, Mittelallalin, Längfluh, Spielboden, Plattjen, Hannig, Stafelwald
Language: German	
Beds: 8,500	
Population: 1,200	Ski schools: Schweizer Skischule Saas-Fee
Health: Doctor and dentist in resort. *Hospital*: Visp (26 km.)	Linked resorts: None
	Season: November to April; summer skiing on glacier
Runs: 80 km.	
Lifts: 26	Kindergarten: *Non-ski*: 3–6 years. *With ski*: none, but ski school from 5 years.

Prices: *Lift pass*: 6 days Sfr. 190 (children Sfr. 115). *Ski school*: Group Sfr. 18 for half-day; private Sfr. 35 per hour.

RATINGS

Skiing Conditions	Snow Conditions	For Beginners	For Intermediates	For Advanced Skiers	For Children	Après-Ski	Other Sports	Value for Money
7	8	6	8	7	7	8	8	7

THE RESORT

Lying in its own valley at the eastern end of the Rhône valley, Saas-Fee is often spoken of as a miniature version of neighbouring Zermatt. The comparison is useful because, like Zermatt, Saas-Fee is a car-free village steeped in mountain tradition. Unlike Zermatt, Saas-Fee is directly accessible by road, and cars can be left in the covered parking areas at the end of the village. The village itself can be rather dark, particularly in the early part of the season. Because it sprawls over the hillsides, visitors must be prepared to do quite a bit of walking. There are plenty of good hotels here, offering impeccable Swiss service and hospitality.

THE SKIING

The main ski area here is Felskinn/Mittelallalin. To get to the start of the Felskinn cable car (for which there are often bad queues—even in low season), you first have to take a drag lift from the edge of the village. At the top of the Felskinn cable car is the start of the Metro Alpin, Saas-Fee's celebrated underground express funicular. There are seldom bad queues here, and if you have to wait a bit you can always admire the murals on the tunnel walls. At the top of the Metro Alpin is Mittelallalin (3500 m.), where there is

a revolving restaurant offering spectacular views and rather less spectacular (but adequate) food.

Before its present slogan "Pearl of the Alps", Saas-Fee used to call itself the "Glacier Village". It is easy to see why when you ski down the beautiful, open pistes on the Feegletscher. You really have a sense of being on a glacier and you can frequently hear it moving. The pistes here have to be redefined regularly to take account of the behaviour of the glacier according to the time of year. This area offers "motorway" skiing of the most exhilarating kind. There are a couple of drag lifts on the glacier; alternatively, you can either take another drag back up to Felskinn and take the Metro Alpin again, ski all the way on back to the village or cruise across to the Längfluh ski area. (There is a connection in the opposite direction, from Längfluh to the Feegletscher by the Fee-Chatz, a kind of snow-cat bus service.)

The Längfluh section offers some good red and black runs, and on the way down to the village a stop at the Gletscher-Grotte café hidden away in the woods beside the piste is recommended. The slopes down from Plattjen offer some steep, open pistes high up and some interesting paths lower down. The Hannig area is for beginners and intermediates, and there are good nursery slopes close to the village.

APRÈS-SKI

There are plenty of cosy, atmospheric bars in Saas-Fee, including the Fee Pub, the Pic Pic and the Walliser Stübli. The Hotel Dom has a restaurant specializing in all kinds of *rösti*, while the Schäferstube, a short uphill walk towards Hohnegg, is a charming rustic place whose speciality is a fondue in which the meat is cooked in wine; the Vieux Chalet concentrates on all the other varieties of fondue. The Fletschhorn is a longish walk out of town, but has an excellent reputation for gourmet food. In the way of discos, the Sans Souci suits the younger crowd, while older people prefer the Walliserhof.

OTHER ACTIVITIES

Saas-Fee has one of the most impressive and modern sports centres in the Alps, which includes a swimming pool, indoor tennis and fitness centre. There is skating and curling on natural rinks, 8 km. of cross-country trails, 20 km. of hiking paths and, if conditions are right, tobogganing.

The Saaser Museum gives a fascinating glimpse into the lives and living conditions of people in this area in years gone by.

ST. MORITZ

Access: *Nearest airport*: Zurich (4 hrs.). *By road*: N13 motorway, exit Chur, then via Julier-Pass. *By rail*: station in St. Moritz.
Tourist Office: CH-7500 St. Moritz. Tel. (082) 3 31 47

Altitude: 1856 m. *Top*: 3304 m.	Ski areas: Corviglia, Piz Nair, Marguns
Language: German, Romansh	
Beds: 12,750	Ski schools: Schweizer Skischule St. Moritz, Schweizer Skischule Suvretta, Schweizer Skischule Palace
Population: 6,000	
Health: Doctors, dentists and fracture clinic in resort. *Hospital:* Samedan (6 km.)	
	Linked resorts: None
Runs: 80 km. (350 km. in Oberengadin)	Season: End November to mid-April; summer skiing on glacier
Lifts: 26 (61 in Oberengadin)	Kindergarten: *Non-ski*: 3–12 years. *With ski*: 4–12 years.

Prices: *Lift pass*: 6 days Sfr. 190 (children Sfr. 140). *Ski school*: Group Sfr. 28 for half-day (children Sfr. 20); private Sfr. 50 per hour.

RATINGS

Skiing Conditions	Snow Conditions	For Beginners	For Intermediates	For Advanced Skiers	For Children	Après-Ski	Other Sports	Value for Money
7	6	5	7	6	6	8	8	7

ST. MORITZ

THE RESORT

Although it is not an attractive place to look at—it is a farrago of countless architectural styles spread around the mountainside—St. Moritz is a beautiful place to look out from. There are spectacular views across the frozen lake, on which horse racing and polo take place, to the mountains beyond. The resort gets the sun for much of the day and the "champagne air" claim does not seem entirely bogus. With an abundance of smart hotels and chic shops, the atmosphere in the resort is more that of a town than a village.

THE SKIING

The main St. Moritz ski area is Corviglia. (A local pass covers this area, but if you want to go further afield you will need the full Engadine pass.) Initial access up as far as Corviglia itself is via a funicular. At the top of this funicular lies La Marmite, which is, gastronomically speaking, the finest mountain restaurant in the Alps. You need to book a table and fill your wallet beforehand. Specialities include caviar and fresh truffles, which do not come cheap. The service, presided over by chef Hartly Mathis, is efficient but unpretentious. Many patrons who come up here do not wear ski gear.

Assuming you can resist the attractions of La Marmite, a cable car, for which there are often queues, will take you up to the summit of Piz Nair at 3057 m. The run from here is long, interesting and quite challenging in places. With one short T-bar connection, this brings you out at the focal point of Marguns, which can be more directly reached via a short run down from Corviglia. There are several drag lifts around here, offering easy intermediate skiing. The same is true of the drag lifts over on the Suvretta side of Corviglia. The Suvretta skiing also links with St. Moritz-Bad, an inferior suburb of St. Moritz itself which lies on the valley floor.

An inconvenient bus ride away from St. Moritz itself is the Corvatsch, which offers the best skiing in the whole of the Engadine. A cable car runs up to 3304 m. on the Corvatsch glacier (summer skiing here, too) and the steep runs down tend to excite even fairly expert skiers. Those with a guide will discover

enormous off-piste possibilities in this area. Lower down there are drag lifts providing agreeable skiing of an intermediate standard through the trees.

APRÈS-SKI

For the most part, après-ski here is smart and expensive. Hanselmann is the best-known tea-time rendezvous, although the back room of Glattfelder is popular for sampling their specialities of tea, coffee and caviar. All the top hotel bars are worth visiting, particularly the Sunny Bar of the Kulm, which is the headquarters

of the predominantly British Cresta Club. All the smart hotels have good, expensive restaurants, but for a cheap dinner in a pleasant atmosphere try the pizzeria of the Chesa Veglia. The most famous and costly nightclub in town is the King's Club in Badrutt's Palace Hotel, but even this can seem quiet outside the jet-set's peak periods. The Steffani Hotel is a good venue for late-night drinking.

OTHER ACTIVITIES

There's a wealth of things to do in St. Moritz, including horse races and golf on the frozen lake, para-gliding and Alpine flights, horse riding, and sleigh excursions to the Roseg and Fex valleys, the famed Cresta Run, not to mention the more usual winter sports: 150 km. of cross-country trails, 120 km. of walks, skating, curling, swimming, tennis, squash and bowling.

The Engadine Museum displays typical furniture, tile stoves and historic weapons in a building based on regional architectural style, while the Segantini Museum exhibits works of the Italian landscape painter Giovanni Segantini (1858–99).

The Glacier Express, a Rhaetian railway, takes you on a 240-km. tour over 291 bridges and through 91 tunnels from St. Moritz to Zermatt. The Bernina Express goes to Tirano in Italy via Poschiavo and Alp Grüm.

VERBIER

Access: *Nearest airport*: Geneva (2½ hrs.). *By road*: N9 motorway, exit Martigny, then Route du Grand-Saint-Bernard via Sembrancher. *By rail*: to Martigny or Le Châble, then bus, or gondola from Le Châble.

Tourist Office: CH-1936 Verbier. Tel. (026) 7 71 81

Altitude: 1500 m. *Top:* 3330 m.	Ski schools: Ecole Suisse de Ski Verbier, Ecole du Ski Fantastique
Language: French	
Beds: 1,500 in hotels, 20,500 in chalets	Linked resorts: Haute-Nendaz, Veysonnaz, Thyon 2000, Les Collons
Population: 1,500	
Health: Doctors, dentist and fracture clinic in resort. *Hospital:* Martigny (27 km.)	Season: December to April; summer skiing on glacier
Runs: 320 km. in 4 Vallées area	Kindergarten: *Non-ski*: 18 months–8 years. *With ski*: 3–10 years.
Lifts: 36 (86 in 4 Vallées area)	
Ski areas: Les Ruinettes, Mont-Fort, Savoleyres, Les Attelas.	

Prices: *Lift pass*: 6 days Sfr. 208 (children Sfr. 104). *Ski school*: Group Sfr. 19 for half-day (children Sfr. 18); private Sfr. 42 per hour.

RATINGS — Skiing Conditions: 9 / Snow Conditions: 8 / For Beginners: 7 / For Intermediates: 8 / For Advanced Skiers: 9 / For Children: 7 / Après-Ski: 8 / Other Sports: 7 / Value for Money: 7

THE RESORT

To look at this pretty resort, comprising mainly chalet-style buildings on a sunny hillside above the Rhône valley, you would be unlikely to guess that Verbier has only existed since the late 1940s. Fortunately, its architects have had more regard for aesthetics than those of many ski resorts. Verbier is conveniently close to Geneva—though transfer by road is much easier than by train—and is popular with weekend skiers from Britain as well as Switzerland. The resort retains a village atmosphere, and life tends to centre around chalets and apartments rather than hotels.

THE SKIING

Verbier certainly offers some of the best skiing in Europe, and the lift pass is priced accordingly. (All good intermediate skiers upwards will find it worthwhile to pay the supplement for the pass that includes the Mont-Fort area.) This skiing is best enjoyed away from peak holiday dates when queues do build up at certain bottlenecks. Getting up the mountain from the Médran station in the village is often a problem. However, the new 150-man cable car (the largest in Switzerland) from La Chaux to Mont-Fort has helped to relieve congestion higher up.

The skiing around Les Attelas, Lac des Vaux and

Les Ruinettes is best suited to good intermediates, although there are some steepish bump runs like Les Fontanays. Tortin is a notorious black mogul run: the first three turns are the worst—after that it gets a little easier. The steep mogul run from the top of Mont-Fort to Col des Gentianes is best left to expert skiers. The runs down the Tortin side of Gentianes are quite taxing, but the one from Gentianes to La Chaux is a good cruise with fantastic views. If the snow cover is very good and you have the stamina, you can ski all the way down to Le Châble (821 m.), below Verbier. For the last stretch, you have to pick your way through orchards and vineyards!

The Savoleyres area, linked to Médran by a bus service, is ideal for intermediates, but on the far side of this area there is a good deal of interesting off-piste skiing on the way to La Tzoumaz. Much of this is through woodland and so is particularly useful in poor light.

The "4 Vallées" circuit, a day tour from Verbier which takes in neighbouring resorts like Haute-Nendaz, is an adventure for intermediates, but is less interesting for better skiers.

Verbier is famous for the extent and variety of its off-piste skiing, but you need to take a guide to discover this. The resort is less famous for its mountain restaurants, but try the upstairs (service) restaurant at Les Ruinettes, as well as Chez Dany, Au Mayen and, in the Savoleyres sector, La Marmotte.

APRÈS-SKI

After skiing, drinks in the Mont-Fort Pub and milkshakes in the Milk Bar are popular. Early evening drinking goes on in the Nelson Pub and La Luge, which also has an excellent steak restaurant in its basement. The Au Fer à Cheval pizzeria is a key meeting point serving cheap food, while the Hotel Rosalp opposite has one of the best restaurants in Switzerland. Late at night, the Farm-Club is the smartest place to go. The very young or impoverished may prefer the Scotch. The cinema shows films in English.

OTHER ACTIVITIES

There are 4 km. of cross-country tracks in Verbier itself, 30 km. of trails down in Le Châble, and 15 km. of walks. The large, modern sports centre offers skating (indoor), curling, swimming, squash and a fitness centre.

The post office organizes bus tours to Aosta in Italy and the Grand Saint Bernard. For trips down to the valley towns of Sion and Martigny, you have to go independently.

VEYSONNAZ

Access: *Nearest airport*: Geneva (2½ hrs.). *By car*: N9 motorway, exit Sion. *By rail*: to Sion, then post bus.
Tourist Office: CH-1993 Veysonnaz. Tel. (027) 27 10 53

Altitude: 1300 m. *Top:* 3304 m.	Ski areas: La Printze
Language: French	Ski schools: Ecole Suisse de Ski Veysonnaz
Beds: 3,000	
Population: 450	Linked resorts: Mayens-de-Riddes, Thyon 2000, Haute-Nendaz, Verbier, Les Collons
Health: Doctor in Thyon 2000. *Hospital:* Sion (14 km.)	
	Season: End November to April
Runs: 320 km. in 4 Vallées area	Kindergarten: *Non-ski*: from 1 year. *With ski*: from 4 years.
Lifts: 35 Veysonnaz-Nendaz (86 in 4 Vallées area)	

Prices: *Lift pass*: 6 days Sfr. 184 (children Sfr. 92). *Ski school*: Group Sfr. 19 for half-day (children Sfr. 17); private Sfr. 38 per hour.

RATINGS

Skiing Conditions	Snow Conditions	For Beginners	For Intermediates	For Advanced Skiers	For Children	Après-Ski	Other Sports	Value for Money
7	6	6	7	5	6	4	5	7

For map see pp. 142–143.

THE RESORT

Veysonnaz is an old Valaisan mountain village which has lately been developed into a ski resort. Fortunately much of the recent building has been in the traditional chalet style. The development has been carefully restricted, and part of the appeal of Veysonnaz is that it has retained its character. In fact, Veysonnaz is the easternmost point in the vast 4 Vallées ski complex, of which the principal and best-known resort is Verbier. Between Veysonnaz and Verbier lies Haute-Nendaz.

THE SKIING

From just outside Veysonnaz, a télécabine rises up above the satellite resort of Thyon 2000. Below this, there are two drag lifts on the slopes down towards Veysonnaz. The area offers pleasant wide-open intermediate skiing and the superb "Piste de l'Ours", used for Swiss downhill championships. There are also drag lifts on the slopes down to Thyon 2000 and these offer access to similarly easy but pleasant skiing.

The most important lift in the Veysonnaz system is in fact the Cheminée drag lift which takes skiers to the start of a long tour, that leads all the way round to Super-Nendaz, the satellite of Haute-Nendaz. En route, the slopes beside the Greppon Blanc I and II chair lifts offer exciting and, depending on snow conditions, challenging descents. From Super-Nendaz a succession of three drag lifts brings you up to the bottom of Tortin (2044 m.). From here there is easy access to the Col des Gentianes/Mont-Fort ski area, for which a supplement must be paid to the ordinary 4 Vallées lift pass. Instead of taking the Mont-Fort cable car, however, skiers can opt for the Tortin télécabine (no supplement payable), ski down to Lac des Vaux, go up to Les Attelas and from there all the way down to Verbier itself. It is worthwhile paying the Mont-Fort supplement to get the very best snow conditions and access to some of the most interesting and longest runs.

Veysonnaz is not really a good choice for expert skiers since the trek to the best skiing (around Mont-Fort, Tortin and Les Attelas) and back again every day would be tiresome. However, it is good

for intermediate skiers wanting to practise in a limited ski area, making perhaps one major long-distance expedition in a week.

APRÈS-SKI

Veysonnaz is a quiet mountain village: definitely not the place to come expecting lively après-ski. However, there is a disco and a limited choice of bars and restaurants.

OTHER ACTIVITIES

These are also limited, with a 10-km. cross-country track, 5 km. of paths for walking, and swimming.

VILLARS

Access: *Nearest airport*: Geneva (1½ hrs.). *By road*: N9 motorway, exit Aigle. *By rail*: to Bex, then connection to Villars, or Aigle, then by bus.
Tourist Office: CH-1884 Villars. Tel. (025) 35 32 32

Altitude: 1300 m. *Top:* 2120 m.

Language: French

Beds: 2,000 in hotels, 8,000 in chalets and apartments.

Population: 2,500

Health: Doctors in resort. *Hospital:* Aigle (14 km.)

Runs: 60 km. (120 km. with Les Diablerets)

Lifts: 24 (48 with Les Diablerets)

Ski areas: Bretaye, Barboleusaz-Les Chaux, Roc d'Orsay

Ski schools: Ecole Suisse de Ski Villars, Ecole de Ski Moderne

Linked resorts: Les Diablerets

Season: Mid-December to mid-April

Kindergarten: *Non-ski*: 3–10 years. *With ski*: 3–10 years.

Prices: *Lift pass*: 6 days Sfr. 155. *Ski school*: Group Sfr. 18 for half-day; private Sfr. 40 per hour.

RATINGS

Skiing Conditions	Snow Conditions	For Beginners	For Intermediates	For Advanced Skiers	For Children	Après-Ski	Other Sports	Value for Money
7	5	6	8	6	7	8	7	7

THE RESORT

Architecturally, Villars is a farrago of styles, but it enjoys a spectacular—and spectacularly sunny—south-west-facing position on the northern side of the Rhône valley, above the towns of Aigle and Bex. The village affords superb panoramic views which

take in Mont Blanc, among many other famous peaks. Although above the Rhône valley, Villars is actually in the canton of Vaud, not the Valais. This means that it is one of the few remaining parts of Switzerland where foreigners can still buy property easily. Partly for this reason, the resort has recently regained popularity with the British and there are many who drive out here and holiday independently. (Villars is one of the closest European resorts to Britain and is also very convenient for Geneva airport—not much more than an hour's drive away when the roads are quiet.)

Villars is a smart, cosmopolitan resort that caters fairly well for all ages and nationalities. The presence of a number of international schools like Aiglon College adds to the resort's United Nations feel. Villars is also a good place for non-skiers, with a fair number of chic shops and the potential for excursions up the mountain by train and also down to towns on Lake Geneva, such as Montreux and Lausanne.

THE SKIING

Villars is most certainly a resort for intermediate skiers rather than experts. The ski area is not enormous, but there is a good variety of pleasant, easy, sunny slopes. The resort now has a useful link with Les Diablerets and its glacier. This obviously extends the range of the skiing, but it does not provide any significantly more difficult runs. The glacier means that some skiing will be available at either end of the season when Villars' own south-facing slopes may not be well covered. Skiing on the glacier lifts, however, requires the purchase of a separate lift ticket, and the glacier has an unfortunate reputation for being frequently closed due to bad weather.

The main Villars skiing area centres around Bretaye (1800 m.) which is reached either by mountain railway from the centre of Villars—this line in fact runs all the way up from Bex in the valley—or by télécabine from the Chesières side of the resort up to Roc d'Orsay (2000 m.) and then a short run down. Chair and drag lifts fan out from here, offering lots of easy intermediate skiing, but also quite a few undemanding off-piste possibilities. There is a more testing off-piste run in the form of the *couloir* at the back of Chaux de Conches, but this is often closed.

The smaller, less interesting Villars ski area rises to Les Chaux (1750 m.) and Croix des Chaux (2020 m.). It does link with Bretaye, but can also be reached by a télécabine from Barboleusaz, which is just above the village of Gryon. The slopes here provide fun intermediate skiing but get an awful lot of sun.

APRÈS-SKI

Villars does not exactly throb by night, but there is a good range of après-ski venues to please all but the most dedicated après-skiers. The choice of restaurants includes Le Peppino in the highly regarded Eurotel and Le Sporting which has a superb list of Swiss wines (many of them coming from vineyards around Villars), as well as cheaper places like La Suisse—ideal for fondues. One of the newest hotels in Villars is the Panorama, which incorporates the Kam Yu, a good but pricey Chinese restaurant, and the New Sam, one of the most lively and sophisticated discos in the Alps with a fantastic light-show. For less affluent disco-goers the alternative is El Gringo.

OTHER ACTIVITIES

These include 30 km. of cross-country tracks, 25 km. of prepared walks, skibob, swimming, skating, curling, tennis, squash and indoor golf, bowling, horse riding and a fitness centre. Villars is well placed for excursions down to Lake Geneva and the towns along its banks.

WENGEN

Access: *Nearest airport*: Zurich (2½ hrs.); Berne (1½ hrs.). *By road*: N6 motorway, exit Spiez, via Interlaken to Lauterbrunnen, then narrow-gauge railway (BOB). *By rail*: to Lauterbrunnen, then BOB to Wengen.

Tourist Office: CH-3823 Wengen. Tel. (036) 55 14 14

Altitude: 1274 m. *Top:* 2320 m.

Language: German

Beds: 2,200 in hotels, 3,500 in apartments and chalets

Population: 1,150

Health: Doctor in resort. *Hospital:* Interlaken (12 km.)

Runs: 80 km. (165 km. in Jungfrau Region)

Lifts: 18 (43 in Jungfrau Region)

Ski areas: Kleine Scheidegg, Männlichen

Ski schools: Schweizer Skischule Wengen

Linked resorts: Grindelwald

Season: November to April

Kindergarten: *Non-ski*: 3–7 years. *With ski*: none, but ski school from 3 years.

Prices: *Lift pass*: 6 days Sfr. 168 (children Sfr. 112). *Ski school*: Group Sfr. 17 for half-day; private Sfr. 38 per hour.

RATINGS

Skiing Conditions	Snow Conditions	For Beginners	For Intermediates	For Advanced Skiers	For Children	Après-Ski	Other Sports	Value for Money
7	5	7	8	8	8	8	7	7

THE RESORT

Wengen is quite simply one of the prettiest, most atmospheric ski resorts in Switzerland, indeed in the world. It is an old village, still owned and run by mountain people, but because the British have been coming here ever since skiing was invented, they have a special place in the locals' hearts. There are some grand hotels in Wengen, but this car-free resort, dominated by the Eiger and the Jungfrau, still retains the feeling of being a small Alpine village, almost cut off from the rest of the world and reached only by a fantastic mountain railway.

THE SKIING

Wengen is the central resort in the vast Jungfrau ski area, which also includes Grindelwald and Mürren. The Jungfrau pass is only marginally more expensive than the standard Wengen (Kleine Scheidegg/Männlichen) pass and is worth the extra for skiers who want to explore the whole region. A day-trip to Mürren is a bit of an expedition, but quite fun all the same.

There is lots of good skiing for advanced intermediates in Wengen, as well as a few more-taxing runs for experts. As there are nursery slopes right in the middle of the village, this is an ideal place to learn. Much of the best skiing is reached by the mountain railway which runs from the centre of town up to Kleine Scheidegg (2061 m.), with several stops en route. From here you can follow the famous World Cup Lauberhorn course. There are pretty runs through the trees down to Innerwengen (1300 m.), as well as some short, demanding runs beside the Innerwengen chair lift and, fur-

ther up, beside the aptly named Bumps drag lift. There is also good skiing beside the Wixi chair lift. The best restaurant for lunch in this sector is the Jungfrau Hotel at Wengernalp, but this stylish place by the railway tracks is so popular with the British and others that you need to reserve your table in advance.

The Grindelwald/Grund slopes can be reached either by skiing down the other side from Kleine Scheidegg or by taking the Männlichen cable car up from Wengen village. (To return to the Wengen side, however, you need to take the Grindelwald train up to Kleine Scheidegg.) The skiing on this side consists mainly of broad, open pistes, but there are also some pretty woodland paths, such as that down to the middle railway station at Brandegg. It is often better to use the chair and drag lifts higher up in this area, as there can be bad queues for the long télécabine up from Grund to Männlichen.

APRÈS-SKI

Après-ski tends to begin on the mountain: Mary's Café or the Café Oberland are both good places to stop for a restorative alcoholic coffee on the final run home. The Eiger Bar, the Pizzeria Bar of the Victoria Lauberhorn and the Tanne Bar are all popular drinking places. Most eating out must be done in hotel restaurants. The Carrousel nightclub at the Regina Hotel is the smartest late-night meeting place. One wall is all glass, giving fantastic views over the village and the mountains. The cinema shows a good variety of films, mainly in English.

OTHER ACTIVITIES

There's a 12-km. cross-country track in the Lauterbrunnen valley and 20 km. of walks. For the rest, you can choose from skating and curling on artificial and natural rinks, sleigh-rides, skibob, tobboganing, hang-gliding, and swimming (in hotels).

The railway excursion from Kleine Scheidegg through the Jungfrau mountain to the Jungfraujoch (3454 m.) is not included on the lift pass but should excite even the most jaded sightseers.

ZERMATT

Access: *Nearest airport*: Geneva (5 hrs.); Zurich (4–4½ hrs.). *By road*: N6 motorway, exit Spiez, road to Kandersteg, car-train to Visp; or N9 motorway and E2 to Visp. Then by road to Täsch and by train to Zermatt. *By rail*: express to Visp, then connection to Zermatt.

Tourist Office: CH-3920 Zermatt. Tel. (028) 66 11 81

Altitude: 1620 m. *Top:* 3820 m.	Ski areas: Schwarzsee/Klein Matterhorn, Sunegga/Rothorn, Gornergrat/Stockhorn
Language: German	
Beds: 18,300	
Population: 4,100	Ski schools: Schweizer Ski-schule Zermatt
Health: Doctors and dentist in resort. *Hospital:* Visp (28 km.)	Linked resorts: Cervinia (Italy)
	Season: End November to end April; summer skiing on glacier
Runs: 150 km.	
Lifts: 37	
	Kindergarten: *Non-ski*: 1 month–8 years. *With ski*: from 4 years.

Prices: *Lift pass*: 6 days Sfr. 222 (children Sfr. 111). *Ski school*: Group Sfr. 155 for 6 days; private Sfr. 110 for half-day.

RATINGS

Skiing Conditions	Snow Conditions	For Beginners	For Intermediates	For Advanced Skiers	For Children	Après-Ski	Other Sports	Value for Money
9	8	5	8	9	6	9	8	7

ZERMATT

THE RESORT

Dominated by Switzerland's most famous landmark—the Matterhorn—Zermatt is certainly the country's best all-round ski resort. Moreover, there are many, many skiers who would have no hesitation in naming Zermatt as the Best Ski Resort in the World. Partly thanks to the Matterhorn, but also thanks to the lack of cars and the resort's great sense of tradition, Zermatt has a special, alluring atmosphere that is superior to that of any other resort in Switzerland.

From the moment you arrive at the main station by mountain railway and catch your first glimpse of the ever-changing aspect of the Matterhorn, it is clear that you are in one of the world's great mountain villages. Indeed, despite all the development in recent years, Zermatt has succeeded in retaining a village atmosphere—perhaps because this is a resort that is as busy in summer as in winter and has a substantial year-round population. In fact, the community is still essentially controlled by half a dozen local families. Many are hoteliers, and Zermatt has some of the finest luxury hotels in the Alps, like the Mont Cervin, the Zermatterhof and the Monte Rosa. But even hotels in the middle and lower brackets are excellently run.

THE SKIING

There are three main ski areas in Zermatt, but they do not interconnect perfectly and each system starts from a different point in the village. It is therefore impossible to stay near all three bottom lift stations. A certain amount of walking in ski boots with your skis on your shoulder is always necessary in Zermatt, but few visitors really mind this, especially as everybody else is walking in ski boots with skis over their shoulders. As far as interconnecting between the systems is concerned, the only real problem is that you cannot go from the Klein Matterhorn sector into the Gornergrat sector—you *can* go from Riffelalp in the Gornergrat sector to Furri on the Klein Matterhorn side. Otherwise, interconnections between the ski areas are pretty good. In practice, each of the areas is large enough to keep an expert skier busy for a whole day.

The Schwarzsee/Trockener Steg/Klein Matterhorn system starts at the far end of the village and rises up to 3820 m., offering the highest skiing in Europe and excellent summer skiing. The highest cable-car station is an amazing piece of engineering being actually built into the rock of the Klein Matterhorn. It is nearly always very cold up here, even in spring, but the low temperatures also mean that the snow stays in excellent condition. The slopes at the top of the Klein Matterhorn are actually fairly gentle and are well suited to early intermediates. However, below Trockener Steg the slopes become steeper and more demanding. (Incidentally, from the top of Klein Matterhorn it is possible to ski down to Cervinia in Italy. The runs are not difficult and good intermediates can manage them easily. You have to pay a supplement to use the lifts back up from the Italian side.)

There is some testing skiing beside the Garten drag lift, but the most demanding skiing on this sector is over by the Hörnli drag lift which gives access to steep narrow runs like Mamatt and Tiefbach. All the runs from Furgg or Schwarzsee to Furri involve at least some black sections except for the red Weisse Perle.

Furgg–Furi and Schwarzsee–Furi are both long, testing black pistes. From Furi to the bottom there are easy paths past appealing restaurants like Zum See and Blatten.

The Riffelberg/Gornergrat/Stockhorn sector is generally reached by the slow and ancient Gornergrat mountain railway, which can take anything up to an hour to reach the summit of Gornergrat. All the runs leading directly down from Gornergrat are blue, giving plenty of opportunity for "motorway" skiing. From Gornergrat there is a two-stage cable car to Stockhorn (3405 m.) via Hohtälli. There is a huge variety of testing black runs (often not open until early February) from Hohtälli, Rote Nase and Stockhorn, including the legendary Triftji mogul field. Good skiers could scarcely wish for more-challenging terrain—these runs are too steep to be pisted by machines. Most of these runs eventually arrive at Gant, from where there is a télécabine up to Blauherd.

The Sunegga/Blauherd/Unterrothorn sector is easily reached by the miraculous Sunegga express underground funicular which brings skiers up to Sunegga in just five minutes. Queues for this lift are very, very rare—indeed the queueing...
problems that dogged Zermatt a decade or so ago have now largely been eliminated, except at peak holiday periods. From Sunegga there is a télécabine to Blauherd and then a cable car up to Unterrothorn. Over the back of Unterrothorn, there is the fast Kumme chair lift, which offers good snow conditions all winter. From Unterrothorn (3013 m.) there are also some testing black and red runs like the Chamois and Marmotte, which eventually lead right down to resort level. There is also a good, broad run round the other side of Unterrothorn to Gant, passing by the Fluhalp mountain restaurant. This run provides a liaison with the Stockhorn/Gornergrat area. The runs directly from Blauherd to Sunegga are easy, but Blauherd also provides access to the tricky National black run right down to resort level.

Below Sunegga lies the tiny hamlet of Findeln, which contains a cluster of mountain restaurants—there are some 40 in the whole Zermatt area. In Findeln, the best one is Enzo's Hitta, actually one of the finest mountain restaurants in the world.

Switzerland's most famous mountain, the Matterhorn, overlooks the resorts of Zermatt.

APRÈS-SKI

Someone once said "après-ski in Zermatt begins at noon" and they were far from wrong. It is also very much the form, particularly in spring, to linger up the mountain into the early evening. Mountain restaurants such as the Olympia Stubli, on the path down from Sunegga to the resort, are popular drinking places at the end of the day. In the resort itself, the Papperla Pub and—for the rich—Elsie's Bar are also favoured meeting places.

The variety of Zermatt's nightlife is as great as the variety of its skiing. There are bars and restaurants to suit all tastes and budgets. Le Mazot is the best restaurant in town, specializing in superb grilled lamb. The Stockhorn, the Alex Rotisserie Tenne and Chez Gaby are other restaurants with good reputations.

Most hotels in Zermatt of any size have their own bars, often with live entertainment, but the most remarkable hotel in the whole resort is the Hotel de la Poste. The Poste is a vast night-time complex that includes two discos—the Village and the Broken Bar—pasta restaurants and a gourmet restaurant, the Zamoura, which specializes in seafood and has a chic adjacent cocktail bar. The Pink Elephant is an elegant bar where there is often live jazz or other music. Those who cannot find something to please them at night in the Poste can always try the smart Hotel Alex or the Hotel Pollux for entertainment.

OTHER ACTIVITIES

Because there are trains up the mountain, this is a good resort for non-skiers, who can easily get up the mountain to meet skiing friends for lunch.

In addition, there is a whole range of other sporting activities available: 25 km. of cross-country tracks, 30 km. of cleared walking paths, skating on natural ice rinks, curling and swimming (14 in hotels open to the public and one salt-water pool), squash, tennis, and a fitness centre in the Hotel Christiania..

There is also a fascinating Alpine museum and a cemetery dedicated to souls claimed by the mountains.

BERLITZ SKI-INFO

An A-Z Summary of Practical Information, Facts and Advice

CONTENTS

Accommodation (hotels, pensions, chalets, apartments)
Airports
Booking
Children
Climate
Clothing and Accessories
Driving (entering Switzerland, driving regulations, speed limits, motoring organizations, road conditions, breakdowns, fuel and oil, mountain roads, Alpine passes, tunnels, parking, roofracks, winter tyres and snow chains)
Entry Requirements
Equipment
Getting There (air, coach, rail, cross-Channel ferry)
Health and Medical Care
Holidays
Insurance
Lifts (lift passes)
Money Matters (currency, traveller's cheques, credit cards, cash, banks and currency exchange)
Prices
Ski School
Snow Conditions
Tourist Information Office

A ACCOMMODATION

Hotels. The Swiss are the world's greatest hotel-keepers, and some of the finest examples of their craft are to be found in the country's ski resorts. Whether you choose a basic one-star or a luxurious five-star hotel, you are almost certain to get good service and good value for money. Many of the more up-market hotels have their own swimming pools, saunas and even massage facilities.

Pensions are small hotels/guest houses generally run by a resident family.

Chalets. A catered chalet holiday is a very popular alternative to hotel accommodation. A tour operator normally takes over a chalet-style residence and provides it with English-speaking staff. You can choose from a cosy six-some to a jumbo chalet, which is more like a hotel, often with its own bar and discotheque. Chalets can sometimes be taken on a self-catering basis.

Apartments. These, too, can be anything from a studio not large enough to swing a cat in to luxury accommodation with en suite bathrooms and south-facing balconies. If all you want to do is ski hard all day and crash out at night after dining in a local restaurant, a tiny studio is fine. On the whole, however, self-catering apartments in Switzerland are more generous in size than those in France. It's easiest to book through a tour company and claim a reduction if not using the flight or through private owners (also good for non-catered chalets) via small ads in skiing magazines.

AIRPORTS

The main airports in Switzerland are Geneva (serving resorts in the Portes du Soleil area and in the whole of the cantons of Vaud and Valais) and Zurich (serving the remainder of the country). Both these airports have an integrated mainline railway station, so transfer onwards by train is very straightforward.

For a small extra charge you can check your luggage through from the airport's railway station to your destination. The same applies in reverse, and in many cases you can check luggage through from your resort to your home airport.

Taxis are available from airports to resorts, but they are expensive and in most cases it makes sense to use trains and connecting mountain railway or bus services. Car hire can be organized in the arrivals hall.

Special arrangements usually apply to those travelling on tour operator charter flights, particularly at the departure stage, when check-in may take place away from the main terminal.

During the skiing season, a special office is set up by a British agency, the TOCC (Tour Operators' Centralized Communication), at Geneva airport to coordinate the affairs of tour operator groups passing through the airport. The English-speaking staff will also help and advise independent skiers, although their main purpose is to ensure that transfer of tour operator groups from plane to resort and vice versa goes as smoothly as possible. They also handle medical repatriations.

Flights to Berne airport can be useful, particularly for the Bernese Oberland.

BOOKING (See also INSURANCE.)

The market leaders in the ski tour operator business are best booked through a travel agent, though some smaller companies will sell direct to the client.

If you are booking through a tour operator, air transport and transfer by coach to your resort are included in the cost of your holiday. Some will even offer you free or discounted travel from your home to the departure airport, especially if there is a group booking. These companies get very good flight deals, so if you make your own way, but take their accommodation, you won't find you've made much of a saving. Some operators offer a coach alternative—cheaper, but also long and tiring.

Wading through tour operator brochures can sometimes be more confusing than helpful, until you know what to look for, though even the most experienced sometimes find they haven't got what they want. Books exist solely on the subject

B of finding the right holiday to suit your needs and budgets. Another idea is to look through the specialist magazines, especially around September and October, as they usually carry out detailed analyses.

Package tours cater for everyone—from all-inclusive learn-to-ski weeks (travel, accommodation, lift pass, equipment hire, tuition) to advanced off-piste powder weeks. Book with one of the giants for competitive prices in hotels or self-catering. Go through a specialist company for something different and personal service.

Many companies offer early-booking and full-payment discounts (brochures come out already in summer) and most 1 free place for every 10 bookings, and discounts for children. Most companies now offer a snow guarantee whereby they transport you free of charge to a nearby resort with snow or refund you for every ski day lost. Read the small print at the end of the brochure and make sure you will get a full refund should the company cancel your trip, as well as fair refund if you have to back out; percentage refunds decrease the closer cancellation is to departure date. The tendency is for larger operators to give a better deal than the smaller ones.

Other interesting features in the brochures are special January reductions and free airport car parking. A few companies cater for long weekends and 10/11 night options and others offer gourmet chalet or luxury hotel accommodation.

You can, of course, arrange your holiday independently, but it works out cheaper in the long run to travel package.

C CHILDREN

More and more parents are taking even tiny babies on skiing holidays. The modern idea is that the sooner the child is introduced to the snow environment the better, it being allowed to "grow up" on skis.

Several tour companies have recognized this market potential and provide English nannies. Many others have special family chalets, nanny weeks and crêche facilities. There is a great range of different reductions for children, so look out for good deals—and even free places.

Even if you don't take a special package, by selecting the right resort you can still find freedom. Make sure the local kindergarten caters for youngsters in the right age group. They will be looked after all day, and older ones will play in the snow and start learning to ski. From the age of six (sometimes younger), children can go to ski school. Language isn't usually a problem. Some ski schools take the children all day and supervise lunch, others finish at midday. Resorts geared towards catering for families often offer nursery and baby-sitting facilities in hotels.

Obviously children, particularly babies, will feel the cold, so do take adequate clothing. All-in-one padded suits are best, with a vest and a couple of lightweight jumpers underneath, mittens (attached to the suit or they'll disappear) and always a hat (preferably tied on), as well as a hood which insulates the ears well. Eyes and skin must be well protected. Ordinary sunglasses will not do. Invest in a pair with 100 per cent UV (ultra-violet) and IR (infra-red) block. Use extra high protection sun block (Factor 15). Cold air dries the skin; various kinds of cream exist to prevent this.

Take with you any specialist items, food, toiletries, etc., which you might not find abroad.

CLIMATE

The climate in the Alps is extremely changeable. Recent Decembers have been warm and sunny, but disappointing with regard to snow cover. Watch out for frostbite in January and February (see HEALTH AND MEDICAL CARE), especially at the top of the mountain; it can be pleasant at resort level and a raging blizzard on high. March and April can be gloriously hot and sunny. Good snow lasts into April at higher resorts. Lower ones tend to get patchy in late March, south-facing slopes become slushy by midday and it has been known to rain! When it rains in the resort, it's snowing higher up the mountain, so all is not lost.

The higher the resort the colder it will be, but the sun will be strong when it's out. North-facing slopes will obviously be colder than south-facing ones because they don't get the sun. Take into account the wind-chill factor, especially if skiing at speed.

C While skiing, you are often in the clouds. If it is foggy in the village, don't despair. You may well climb way above it to sunny slopes and look down on a sea of mist. Conversely, sometimes it's better to stick to lower slopes because the peak is in cloud.

The snow never melts in high glacial mountain areas. Summer weather can be equally deceptive. A sunny shirts-off day can deteriorate rapidly into arctic conditions. (Remember it is much colder on the glacier than in the village below.)

The resort tourist office usually pins the weather forecast outside for skiers to consult.

Recorded information on weather and snow conditions can be obtained by dialling the following numbers anywhere in Switzerland. Bulletins are in French, German or Italian depending on the language of the area.

>   Weather forecast   162
>   Snow conditions   120

It is possible to obtain these numbers from abroad by dialling the relevant international prefix plus area code. For information on the weather in a particular resort, it is best to phone the local tourist office direct.

CLOTHING AND ACCESSORIES

Be prepared! Due to the vagaries of mountain weather (see CLIMATE) always err on the cautious side. It's better to sweat a bit than die of hypothermia. The outer ski suit can be a one-piece or ski pants (stretchy racing ones or padded salopettes) and a jacket. The advantage of the former is that snow can't get up your back and it's comfortable to wear. Choose a two-piece if you want the jacket to double as après-ski wear or even casual gear back home. The jacket will ideally have a high collar, incorporating a roll-up hood, and close-fitting cuffs. Look closely at the label: Gore-Tex, Entrant and Cyclone are waterproof; Thinsulate and Isodry supply lightweight warmth; Tactel is ICI's great, new waterproof fibre ideal for ski wear.

Several thin layers under your suit provide better insulation than a bulky jersey. Natural fibres—silk, cotton, wool—wick moisture away from the skin. A long-sleeved thermal vest and long johns are essential, with a cotton skiing roll-neck and possibly another thin woollen jumper or a sweatshirt. It really depends on the thermal qualities of your suit, the weather and individual needs. If too hot, you can always take a layer off and tie it round your waist. It helps to carry a rucksack or bumbag to house accessories. You only need to wear one pair of tube-type ski socks (not ribbed).

Mitts are warmer than gloves, but you have to take them off to adjust boots and bindings. Either get leather handwear or Gore-Tex. Carry a pair of silk glove-liners and a silk balaclava just in case—frostbite sets in very quickly. A large percentage of body heat is lost through the head, so have a hat with you always. Headbands are good, too, for keeping the ears cosy.

Goggles and specs are most important. Always take both with you whatever the weather in the valley. A yellow-amber tint gives best definition. Never economize on eyewear. Altitude and reflection off the snow increase damage to the cornea caused by ultra-violet radiation. Make sure the lenses block out damaging UV, and infra-red if possible. Darker lenses are more dangerous because the pupil dilates, allowing more rays in.

Although ski wear has become a fashion commodity, practicality should take precedence over colour and style.

Après-ski. Take loose and comfortable clothing to change into for the evening after the rigours of a day's labours on the slopes. Few hotels observe formal dining requirements, but it's a good idea for men to take a tie in case circumstances demand. Dancing in après-ski boots is difficult, so, if you visit a local discotheque, it's not a bad idea to have a pair of lightweight shoes or slippers tucked into your pocket or bag.

DRIVING

Entering Switzerland. To take your car into Switzerland you will need:

- Your national driving licence
- Car registration papers

D
- Green Card (a recommended but not obligatory extension to your regular insurance policy, making it valid for foreign countries).
- Nationality plate or sticker
- Red warning triangle

In order not to dazzle oncoming traffic at night, you can buy special black tape to mask a portion of the left-hand side of the headlights. These stickers come in sizes to suit your car model and are obtainable from local dealers.

Naturally, you should ensure your car is in excellent working order and likely to stand up to the extreme conditions encountered in mountain driving (and parking). If your car engine is water cooled, make sure you have a good anti-freeze, and a strong solution for the windscreen wash. A tow rope and shovel are recommended.

Driving regulations. As elsewhere on the continent, drive on the right, overtake on the left, yield right-of-way to all vehicles coming from the right (except on roundabouts) unless otherwise indicated. Seat belts are obligatory. If you wear glasses you are required to carry an extra pair.

Speed limits. On the motorways maximum speed is 120 kph (around 75 mph), on other roads 80 kph (50 mph), unless otherwise indicated. In residential areas the speed limit is restricted to 50 kph (about 30 mph).

Motoring organizations. In Switzerland, the TCS (*Touring Club Schweiz/Touring Club Suisse/Touring Club Svizzero*) provides breakdown service, gives information on road conditions and helps tourists. The headquarters are at 9, rue Pierre Fatio, 1211 Geneva 24; tel: (022) 37 12 12.

In Britain consult the Automobile Association (AA), Fanum House, Basingstoke, Hants., tel. (0256) 20123; or the Royal Automobile Club (RAC), P.O. Box 100, RAC House, Lansdowne Road, Croydon, Surrey, tel. (01) 686 2525.

The AA and RAC both produce excellent booklets, *Guide to Motoring Abroad* and *Continental Motoring Guide*. The latter has a section on toll roads and mountain passes. Both also have special insurance schemes for members and non-members. Obtain your Green Card through the AA.

Road conditions. In general roads are good and regularly maintained. A well-developed motorway network links all the big towns. There are no toll gates on Swiss motorways, instead you are required to display a special windscreen sticker, renewable every January, which entitles you to use the country's motorway system for the year. These can be purchased at Swiss border posts, filling stations and post offices or bought in advance from the AA. Hire cars are already equipped with them. Police do carry out spot checks and you risk a heavy fine for not having a sticker.

For details on road conditions, itineraries and other tourist information phone the TCS at (022) 35 80 00—24 hours a day. There is almost always someone there who speaks English.

Breakdowns. Switch on the flashing warning lights and place a warning triangle 50 m. behind your car (150 m. on high-speed roads). Then phone the TCS. It is wise to take out internationally valid breakdown insurance as you will have to pay the full bill for the help of a serviceman or patrolman. On the motorway, you will find emergency telephones at regular intervals. If calling from a public phone box, dial 140.

Fuel and oil. Fuel, increasingly self-service, is available in super (98 octane), unleaded (91 and 95 octane) and diesel. Lead-free fuel is widely available. All grades of motor oils are on sale.

Service-station attendants expect to be tipped. Many filling stations do not accept credit cards, but Eurocheques are welcomed. They often have 24-hour petrol-dispensing systems, which take notes of Sfr. 10 and 20.

Mountain roads. Even in the mountains, winter motoring is not severely restricted. However, you are advised to be extremely cautious, because as well as being steep with continuous hairpin bends, roads are often snow-covered and icy. On difficult stretches, priority is given to postal buses— otherwise to ascending vehicles. Sounding your horn is recommended on blind corners of mountain roads.

There is a special art to driving on ice and in snowy conditions. The golden rule is always to drive more slowly than you think you should. Avoid sharp reactions or sudden braking; it's better to anticipate well in advance, such as keeping a good distance from the car in front (two or three times the normal braking distance). When starting off or going uphill, put the car in the highest possible gear to avoid wheel spin. Never drive in ski or après-ski boots.

To check conditions, phone 163 (recorded information in French, German or Italian depending on the language of the area you are phoning from).

Alpine passes. Some passes close regularly during winter months, others open and close according to prevailing weather conditions. It is best to join a motoring organization (AA or RAC) and ask their advice. They will also give you a number on the continent to call for local advice. You could ask the local tourist office, but they often cannot help with a distant pass.

Tunnels. There are many new ones now open, so bring an up-to-date map with you. A toll may be charged. If you are driving from Britain to Switzerland, you may not have to use a tunnel at all. The Loetschberg Tunnel from Kandersteg to Goppenstein links the Bernese Oberland (northern slopes of the Alps) with the Valais (southern slopes).

Parking. Some resorts do not allow cars to circulate and, although you can drop luggage off, you have to leave the car in a special parking area. Snow often covers the parking restrictions on the road surface, so look around for the corresponding post or you could find your vehicle towed away and a hefty fine to pay to recover it.

Try to park your car in a place where it, or at least the engine, will be sheltered from the wind and the handbrake can be left off to avoid it being frozen on. But then don't forget to leave the car in gear! Pull windscreen wipers away from the glass.

Roofracks. Skiing luggage, if you have all the equipment, can be excessive. Boxes which fit onto the roof are excellent (though expensive) and protect skis and other belongings from the elements. Regular ski roofracks cost less and can also be hired from some ski-hire shops or the AA (Dover branch only).

Winter tyres and snow chains. You can get your car fitted with winter tyres which grip better than regular tyres, but even these may not be good enough for some snowy mountain roads. Studded tyres are subject to restrictions: there is a speed limit of 80 kph (you should also display a disk stating the maximum speed of the vehicle); they can only be used from 1st November to 31st March; and they are prohibited on all motorways.

On many mountain roads it is obligatory to have chains in the car even if conditions do not necessitate their use. These come in various tyre sizes and vary in price usually according to sophistication and ease of handling. Major ski shops hire them out, as do the AA (Dover branch only) and most specialist garages in Switzerland. Cheaper still, buy them from hypermarkets in mountain areas. Practise putting on your chains *before* you get stuck in heavy snow.

ENTRY REQUIREMENTS

Most visitors, including citizens of Britain, the United States, Canada, Australia and New Zealand, need only a valid passport to enter Switzerland. British subjects can use the simplified Visitor's Passport. Without further formality, you are generally entitled to stay for up to 90 days.

The following chart shows what main duty-free items you may take into Switzerland and, when returning home, into your own country.

Into:	Cigarettes	Cigars	Tobacco	Spirits	Wine
Switzerland*	200 or (400)	50 or (100)	250 g. (500 g.)	1 l.	and 2 l.
Australia	200 or	250 g. or	250 g.	1 l.	or 1 l.
Canada	200 and	50 and	900 g.	1.1 l.	or 1.1 l.
Eire	200 or	50 or	250 g.	1 l.	and 2 l.
N. Zealand	200 or	50 or	250 g.	1.1 l.	and 4.5 l.
S. Africa	400 and	50 and	250 g.	1 l.	and 2 l.
U.K.	200 or	50 or	250 g.	1 l.	and 2 l.
U.S.A.	200 and	100 and	**	1 l.	or 1 l.

* The figures in parentheses are for non-European visitors only.
** A reasonable quantity.

E EQUIPMENT (See also CLOTHING AND ACCESSORIES.)

First of all you need to decide whether to buy or hire and then whether to do so at home or in the resort. If you're a beginner, there is no point in buying skis and boots. Once you have the bug and have reached intermediate standard, you might consider getting your own gear. If you hire in Britain, you'll get the chance to try the boots on a dry slope (or at least wear them round the house), and if they hurt or are loose, change them. On the other hand you will be burdened with extra baggage. You can hire from Airport Skis (Gatwick and Manchester), who will reimburse you if the boots don't fit and you have to re-hire in the resort.

Hiring in the resort could waste a lot of time. Everyone rushes to the hire shop on the first morning, the staff may be overworked, communication might be tricky and you could be ill-fitted. If not totally satisfied with your equipment, take it back and change it. Painful boots and unsuitable skis can ruin a holiday.

Boots should fit snugly and the heel should not lift up when leaning forward. Don't do them up too tightly (it will cut the circulation and be very painful) nor pad out boots that are too big with several layers of socks. Rear-entry boots are easiest to deal with for a beginner. Classic clip boots give more control to expert skiers.

Your forearm should be parallel with flat ground when holding the pole. To test this, turn the pole upside down and grip it below the basket. You can either choose a pole with a sword grip (easy to use) or strap (less likely to get lost in a fall). Most poles have a combination of both.

Opinions on the right length of ski follow fashion trends. Much depends on the type of ski (e.g. recreational, special, competition), and the weight and ability of the skier. If you get a ski which is either too long or too stiff it will spoil your skiing. Beginners should go for flexible, relatively short skis for easy turning. Stiff, long skis require precision technique, but will hold icy slopes better. Flexible skis, however, perform best in powder snow.

Buyers and hirers alike should ensure that the shop technician has regulated the binding (DIN) setting to suit the weight and ability of the skier.

Finally, look after your skis. Get them hot-waxed every two days (even hire skis) for optimum performance. Keep the edges sharp to maintain control on hard-packed snow. Save money by learning how to do it yourself.

GETTING THERE (See also BOOKING.)

Air. If booking independently, you need to decide whether to travel by scheduled or charter flight. Tour operators often offer charter-flight seats at lower fares than those on scheduled services. However, scheduled services are also discounted through flight sales agencies close to the date of departure. These agencies advertise in national newspapers and are often good for last-minute bargains. Normally, though, there is a bewildering array of tickets for scheduled services, with prices for the same class of seating varying greatly depending on when you book and how long you want to stay.

If you are travelling on a tour operator's charter flight, there may well be space on their connecting coach, so buying a seat right through to the resort will save you trouble.

Coach. There is a regular coach service from London Victoria coach station to Geneva. Call (01) 730 0202 for details.

Rail. This is a good choice if travelling independently, especially if going to a resort either with, or close to, a railway station, as it can cut transfer times considerably. You can also take a night train, book a sleeper, have a nice dinner and wake up in the Alps. On arrival, there are buses which meet the train and transport you to the resort. There are daily direct train services from Ostend (Belgium) to Chur for Arosa, or Landquart, giving connections to Klosters and Davos. For other destinations in Switzerland, you will need to change in Paris or Basle. The TGV has daily services from Paris to Geneva and Lausanne.

If travelling with skis, you are advised to register these three to four days before departure at the Registered Baggage Office at Victoria Station. You will need to take your ticket along with you.

G For information on rail travel in Europe, contact the European Rail Travel Centres to be found at major railway stations in most British cities. They can help with timetables, prices and bookings.

Cross-Channel Ferries. There are plenty of ferry crossings each day. Remember sea conditions tend to be rougher in winter. A trip by Hovercraft is quicker and only slightly more expensive, but crossings are occasionally cancelled due to high seas. Some ferry lines offer special ski-package rates. Pick up a *Travel Agency Car Ferry Guide* for details.

H HEALTH AND MEDICAL CARE

Even minor skiing injuries can turn out to be very expensive to treat, and a major accident could ruin you if your medical insurance were not adequate (see INSURANCE).

Provided that you have some sort of insurance, very few doctors in Switzerland insist on being paid in cash on the spot. Most will provide credit, and there are arrangements between the insurance fraternity and doctors abroad for direct payments.

Make sure you get official receipts for everything: rescue service, doctor's or hospital fees, chemist prescriptions. Put in a claim as soon as you get home. There's usually a deadline.

Medical attention is not, of course, limited to traumatic skiing injuries. A nasty cold, flu or stomach upset may necessitate a visit to the doctor, although the local chemist (look for the green cross symbol) may be able to suggest a suitable remedy.

Mountain weather is deceptive (see CLIMATE), and not taking the correct precautions or being adequately dressed (see CLOTHING AND ACCESSORIES) can have serious repercussions. Here are a few of the hazards and what to do if the worst happens:

Altitude sickness. Altitude alone affects many people. Mild altitude sickness experienced at around 3000 m. includes severe headache, nausea and dizziness, but symptoms retreat within an hour of returning to base (your local doctor can prescribe a suitable medicament to prevent this).

Sunburn. Even on a cloudy day you can burn. Put plenty of high protection cream (Factor 15) on exposed areas, concentrating on nose, lips, ears. Apply half an hour before going out to enable the skin to absorb it, and reapply often.

Snowblindness occurs when the eyes are not adequately protected. The thin air at high altitude and reflection of the sun off the snow can combine to damage the eyes. The result can be most uncomfortable, somewhat like having sand or grit under the eyelids. If it should happen to you, stay in a darkened room and bathe the eyes with an eye lotion. Normal sight will return, but the cornea may suffer permanent damage.

Frostbite is when body tissue actually freezes. First signs are white patches on the face (especially nose and ears) and extremities and a total loss of sensation, even of cold. Usually, if the frostbite is on an exposed part of the body, it is a companion who first notices. If it is not too far advanced, placing, for instance, a warm hand over the affected area or rewarming numb and icy fingers under the armpits will be sufficient to bring back sensation. *Never* rub a frostbitten part with snow. More advanced frostbite leads to blistering, and the area turns a greyish-blue. These are very serious symptoms and immediate expert medical treatment is vital.

Hypothermia is the dangerous lowering of the body temperature. Symptoms are somnolence, apathy and lack of coordination, gradually leading to loss of consciousness. It is particularly common in avalanche victims, but can also be the result of insufficient nourishment, combined with extreme cold, high winds or wet. Again, it is the quick reaction of a companion that can avert more dangerous consequences. Get the victim warm, by putting on extra clothes or a covering—a hat, windjackets, sleeping bags or space blankets—that shield from the elements and conserve body heat. Huddling together or sharing body warmth can also be effective. If the victim is fully conscious, administer warm drinks. *Don't* give alcohol, it accelerates loss of body heat; and *don't* encourage the victim to "move around to get warm".

H Injury on the mountain. Place crossed skis about 15 m. above the victim, ensure he is as warm and as comfortable as possible. Send a good skier to the nearest lift station: the attendant will radio the piste patrol, who are qualified to assess and deal with the injuries and transport the casualty to the doctors or ambulance. They will also decide whether a helicopter rescue is necessary. Keep in mind that the piste patrol are not necessarily responsible for the safety and rescue of off-piste skiers.

The international distress signal in the mountains is six shouts or whistles a minute, followed by a minute's silence. Three calls or whistles a minute with a minute's silence is the reply.

HOLIDAYS

The busiest times in Swiss resorts are New Year and Easter. Christmas itself is not too overcrowded, as many families do not head for the mountains until Boxing Day (December 26) or later. Swiss schools break up for a week in February. Exact dates vary according to canton, but this is always a busy time on the slopes. French half-term holidays in February also affect Swiss resorts, particularly those close to the French border.

I INSURANCE (See also BOOKING and HEALTH AND MEDICAL CARE.)

Many tour operators insist that you take their insurance (partly to ensure you are adequately covered), so check it out well and if necessary take out additional coverage independently. Never economize on insurance. Ideally, your winter travel insurance will cover you fully for the following eventualities:

- cancellation or curtailment
- loss or theft of baggage en route, belongings in the resort
- loss or theft of personal money
- breakage of equipment
- illness
- accident on or off the slopes
- rescue service
- transport home

- third party or personal liability, i.e., damage done by you to someone else or to their property

Useful extras:

- missed departure, due to car accident or breakdown or failure of public transport to deliver you to your departure point on time (provided reasonable time has been allowed)
- facility for a friend or relative to stay on in the resort with you if you can't travel immediately, or travel with you on a flight other than the one intended on your package deal
- loss of earnings due to the effects of an injury resulting from your ski accident
- refund on lift pass for every ski day lost through injury

Look closely at the "exclusion clauses" which state the circumstances in which an insurance company won't settle a claim. On each claim there is usually an "excess", which is the difference between what the insurance company will pay and the amount the claimant actually lost. The amount of excess varies from policy to policy.

LIFTS

New and more efficient lift systems are being introduced all the time as more and more skiers want to get up the mountain faster than ever.

Drag or tow lifts. These pull you up the mountain on your skis. One type consists of a saucer-sized disc or "button" which you slip between your legs and place behind your bottom. First-timers should remember *not* to sit down, to keep their skis parallel and to relax as much as possible. If you sit down, the elastic wire attached to the disk will give way under your weight and you will fall over. Your first time on a tow lift can be an unnerving experience, but most lift operators are sympathetic and will slow down the lift and help you on if you manage to communicate your fears to them.

It is fair to say that T-bars, which pull up two people at a time, are universally unpopular. It helps to pick a partner the same size! Tips for riding them well include leaning inwards and keeping the outer ski slightly forwards.

Chair lifts have improved in leaps and bounds over the years, going from single chairs right up to four-seater express lifts which slow down to let you on, then accelerate off at breakneck speed. Advantages: you don't need to take off your skis, so they are quick and easy, and it's pleasant to sit and relax on a sunny day. They are also a good way down from the higher slopes if the low ones are balding or difficult to ski for other reasons. Disadvantages: it can be freezing on a chair lift (some have built-in covers to wrap around you as you ascend); if it's windy they close them down, but on the odd occasion when you're going up on one just before the wind is considered too strong to operate it, the ride can be most uncomfortable; they have a habit of stopping and bouncing mid-route.

Télécabines (often called "eggs" or "bubbles") are little cabins varying from four- to eight-seater express, which you sit in, placing skis in a rack outside. They take you way up the mountain in some comfort, and you are protected from the elements. They, too, can be closed in strong winds.

Cable cars have reached mammoth proportions over the years. You stand in them, holding your skis. They can carry over 150 skiers at a time. Every new one installed takes a few extra skiers, so the resort can boast the biggest cable car for a while.

Funiculars and rack-and-pinion mountain railways are still much used for transporting skiers uphill in some of the older Swiss resorts. Compared with more modern systems, however, they are fairly slow. In Zermatt and Saas-Fee, there are modern high-speed underground funiculars.

Lift passes. Choosing the right type of lift ticket to suit your needs can be difficult. If you are a beginner, there is no need to get a pass for the whole area. Some resorts do not charge for the nursery lifts. A good system for beginners is the punch card. You purchase a card with so many points, and each lift is worth a certain number which the operator punches off the card. More advanced skiers can either buy a daily lift pass, which is best if you don't plan to ski every day, or a more advantageous block pass—six days for a week's holiday—but you'll need to have a passport-sized photo with you. For the vast interlinked ski areas, you then have the option of a pass covering part of the area or the entire network. In some cases this is so vast, an average intermediate would be hard pushed to cover it in a week. You can always get a local pass and pay a daily supplement to ski to another part of the complex.

Don't forget to ask for a piste map of the area at the lift ticket office. Easy runs are marked green; blue are slightly more tricky; red increasingly so. Blacks are for foolhardy intermediates to attempt, advanced skiers to try and experts to come down looking good. Icy conditions, slushy melting snow, fog or a blizzard naturally make the runs more difficult.

MONEY MATTERS

Currency. The monetary unit of Switzerland is the Swiss franc (abbreviated Sfr or Fr.), divided into 100 centimes. Coins come in denominations of 5, 10 and 20 centimes and ½, 1, 2 and 5 francs. Banknotes: 10, 20, 50, 100, 500 and 1,000 francs.

Traveller's cheques are accepted throughout Switzerland, but always have some ready cash with you, too. Eurocheques are also widely accepted.

Credit cards. Most hotels, restaurants and bigger shops will accept these. Smaller businesses generally prefer cash or cheques.

Cash. Always carry enough cash to cover lunch and drinks on the mountain. If you're in a ski area which spans two countries (like the Portes du Soleil in Switzerland and France), have the other currency with you too, or you will lose a lot on the exchange rate.

Banks and currency-exchange offices. Banks in ski resorts are open longer hours than usual (sometimes until 6 or 7 p.m.) Mondays to Fridays, occasionally on Saturday mornings. Don't forget to take your passport with you. Hotels will exchange currency or traveller's cheques/Eurocheques, but not at as good a rate as the bank. The same goes for paying with traveller's cheques in shops.

P PRICES

In Switzerland prices do not vary as much between resorts as in certain countries, although the smarter resorts will always tend to be slightly more expensive than the lesser-known ones. Supermarket chains offer the best value for food shopping. Swiss wine is good but not cheap. Most supermarkets sell less-expensive foreign table wine. However, the prices of Swiss wines sold in bars (Fendant is the most common white and Dole the most common red) are strictly regulated. Open wines are ordered by the decilitre (one glass or by carafes of 2, 3 or 5 decilitres).

While some cafés will err on the side of blandness, it is very unusual to have a bad meal in Switzerland. On the slopes it is worth seeking out smaller mountain restaurants away from the big lift stations. The ambience may be better and prices may well be lower.

In restaurants and bars in the resorts, generally speaking you get what you pay for. It is a good idea to study the menus posted outside the establishment before making a final choice. Raclettes and fondues (cheese or meat) are usually good value.

Most nightclubs and discos charge entrance fees. Often this includes the price of the first drink. If you are in a group, it is often cheaper to buy a bottle of spirits (supplied with free mixers) than a round of drinks. Some bars have a special (higher) late-night tariff.

Here are some average prices in Swiss francs. Despite the country's low inflation rate, they must be regarded as approximate.

Airport transfer. By train, single: Geneva–Verbier Sfr. 40, Geneva–Zermatt Sfr. 66.

Entertainment. Cinema Sfr. 10–12, admission to discotheque (incl. drink) Sfr. 10–25.

Equipment hire. Skis and boots, Sfr. 90–150 per week.

Cigarettes. Packet of 20 Sfr. 2.70.

Hotels (double room, half-board, with bath, per night, per person). ***** Sfr. 276–460, **** Sfr. 180–420, *** Sfr. 130–300, ** Sfr. 110–200, * Sfr. 70–120.

Kindergarten. Sfr. 200–255 per week.

Meals and drinks. Continental breakfast Sfr. 8–12, mountain lunch Sfr. 12–50, set menu Sfr. 20–30, lunch/dinner in fairly good establishment Sfr. 50–80, coffee Sfr. 2–3, whisky or cocktail Sfr. 10–15, beer/soft drink Sfr. 2.50–3, cognac Sfr. 10–15, bottle of wine (Swiss) Sfr. 22.

Supermarket. Bread (450 grams) Sfr. 2.50, butter (200 grams) Sfr. 3.60, coffee (500 grams) Sfr. 4.20–4.70, milk (litre) Sfr. 1.75, eggs Sfr. 2.80 for six.

SKI SCHOOL

The Swiss Ski School (Ecole Suisse de Ski; Schweizer Skischule) has an excellent reputation and its instructors are trained to a very high standard. In most resorts this will be the only ski school, but some do have other, smaller schools, usually specializing in a particular area like off-piste skiing. Finding English-speaking instructors is not generally a problem in Switzerland.

You can either go into group lessons or take a private instructor. Individual tuition is charged by the hour, half-day or full day. Prices rise inexorably every year. It is very expensive on a one-to-one basis, but you learn extremely quickly. Just one hour a day and you'll be streets ahead of the group pupils by the end of the week. If on holiday with a few friends of similar standard it can be beneficial to share private lessons (instructors will only take up to six people).

More advanced skiers will benefit from occasionally joining class 1 (or even the Competition class), where there is very little hanging around and plenty of fast skiing behind the instructor. Expert skiers take a private instructor if they want to explore the area off piste or perfect skiing in the bumps.

SNOW CONDITIONS (See also CLIMATE)

As already mentioned, early season (December) is a gamble. There has been a lack of snow in recent years, so at this time of year it is best to aim high and go to a summer ski resort where you are sure of glacier skiing. The drawback is

S that it might be cold and there's a certain amount of skiing over rocks which, for beginners, is not necessarily the best introduction to winter-sports holidays. Snow in January is usually crisp, dry and a dream to ski. But it can be bitterly cold. Again not a good choice for a novice. In January and February lower resorts—and these are often the prettier, traditional ones with more atmosphere—are usually snow-sure. February is best if it weren't for the school mid-term break (see Holidays). March is warmer, sunnier and altogether more pleasant. However, it can get patchy on the runs leading down to the village, and sunshine, combined with fewer snowfalls and overnight freezing, results in some icy starts. This is not always the case: metres of powder snow can fall in spring. April is more risky and you should select a high-altitude resort for best conditions.

Pistes are generally hard-packed, as they are bashed down by skiers or special machines as soon as the fresh snow falls. Off-piste refers to areas that are not bashed by machines or skied regularly. You shouldn't leap into this great white wilderness unless you're an expert. Even then, you should make sure you know the mountain, otherwise you can never tell what may be lurking under the snow or round the next bend. If you are at all unfamiliar with the terrain, take an instructor or guide. In particular, take special notice of avalanche warnings (yellow and black checked flag). And don't go off piste on a glacier, there is a danger of crevasses. Remember that if anything should go wrong, patrols are irregular or non-existent away from the pistes. Snow and the mountains may appear innocuous, but they claim many lives every year.

You'll find different types of snow on or off piste. If you thought it was simply white flakes that fell out of the sky, you'll discover differently when skiing.

Powder snow. The proverbial skier's dream: crystals of light, dry snow that cannot be formed into a ball. Off piste you float through it; freshly packed down on piste it is easy to glide over. Not all fresh snow is powder: if the weather is warmer, big, wet flakes will fall and that's not the same thing at all. Beware of avalanches off piste after a heavy snowfall.

Hardpack. This common piste condition results from snow which has been compressed over a few days without a snowfall. Moguls (bumps) form, and icy or even bare patches develop should it not snow again for a while.

Porridge is snow which has been chopped up by skiers. It can refer to fresh snow which has been skied over without being bashed by the piste machines. Or in spring when it is warmer and the sun shines, surface snow softens and the pistes get slushy.

Spring snow (also known as corn snow) is lovely to ski, especially off piste. Smooth, wet snow freezes overnight, and first thing in the morning the texture is like granulated sugar. When the surface has just softened, it develops a sheen. This snow is very easy to ski but sadly short-lived. By lunchtime it has generally become too slushy, but it is good to try monoskiing in.

Windslab is an off-piste condition caused by wind blowing powder snow and depositing it in the lee of the mountain, packing it down hard and seemingly unbreakable. It is very dangerous, as great chunks break away in slab avalanches.

Breakable crust. This happens to fresh snow off piste when the surface melts during the day and freezes overnight. It is very difficult to ski over.

TOURIST INFORMATION OFFICES

The Swiss National Tourist Office, Swiss Centre, New Coventry Street, London W1V 8EE, tel. (01) 734 1921, will provide brochures and give you advice, but does not normally book holidays. Staff are very helpful and they will refer you to local tourist offices in the resorts for specialist advice.

SOME USEFUL EXPRESSIONS (FRENCH)
Equipment

I'd like to hire/buy ... J'aimerais louer/acheter ...
  ski boots des chaussures de ski
  ski poles des bâtons de ski
  skis des skis
What length poles/skis should I have? Quelle longueur de bâtons/skis me faut-il?
Can you adjust the bindings? Pouvez-vous régler mes fixations?
Can you wax my skis? Pouvez-vous farter mes skis?
Can you sharpen the edges? Pouvez-vous aiguiser les carres?
I am a ... Je suis un(e) ...
  beginner débutant(e)
  intermediate skier skieur (skieuse) de niveau moyen
  advanced skier skieur (skieuse) avancé(e)
I weigh ... kilos. Je pèse ... kilos.
My shoe size is ... Je chausse du ...

British	4	5	6	6½	7	8	8½	9	9½	10	11
Continental	37	38	39	40	41	42	43	43	44	44	45

These boots are ... Ces chaussures sont ...
  too big/too small trop grandes/trop petites
  uncomfortable inconfortables
Do you have any rear-entry boots? Avez-vous des chaussures (de ski) qui s'ouvrent à l'arrière?

Problems

My skis are too long/too short. Mes skis sont trop longs/trop courts.
My ski/pole has broken. Mon ski/bâton s'est cassé.
My bindings are too loose/too tight. Mes fixations sont trop lâches/trop serrées.
The clasp on my boot is broken. La boucle de ma chaussure s'est cassée.
My boots hurt me. Mes chaussures me font mal.

Clothing and accessories

bumbag	banane
gloves	gants
goggles	lunettes de ski/goggles
hat	bonnet
headband	bandeau
jacket	veste
mittens	moufles
one-piece suit	combinaison
polo-neck sweater	pull à col roulé
rucksack	sac à dos
ski suit	combinaison (de ski)
ski trousers	fuseau(x)
socks	chaussettes
sun glasses	lunettes de soleil

and don't forget:

lip salve	stick protecteur (pour les lèvres)
sun cream	crème solaire

Lifts and lift passes

I'd like a … lift pass.	J'aimerais un abonnement…
day	journalier
season	pour la saison
week	hebdomadaire
I'd like a book of … lift coupons.	J'aimerais un carnet de … coupons.
ten/twenty/thirty	dix/vingt/trente
Do I need a photo?	Est-ce qu'il me faut une photo?
Could I have a lift-pass holder?	Pourrais-je avoir une pochette pour mon abonnement?
cable car	téléphérique
chair lift	télésiège
drag lift	téléski
gondola	télécabine
Where's the end of the queue?	Où se trouve la fin de la queue?
Can I have a piste map, please?	Puis-je avoir un plan des pistes, s'il vous plaît?

On the piste

Where are the nursery slopes?	Où sont les pistes pour débutants?
Which is the easiest way down?	Quelle est la descente la plus facile?
It's a(n) ... run.	C'est une piste ...
easy/difficult	facile/difficile
gentle/steep	en pente douce/escarpée
green (very easy)	verte (très facile)
blue (easy)	bleue (facile)
red (intermediate)	rouge (moyennement difficile)
black (difficult)	noire (difficile)
The piste is closed.	La piste est fermée.
The piste is very icy.	La piste est très gelée.
... snow	neige...
powder	poudreuse
sticky	lourde
mogul (bump)	bosse
rock	rocher/caillou
tree	arbre
Watch out!	Attention!

Ski school

I'd like some skiing lessons.	J'aimerais prendre des leçons de ski.
group/private	en groupe/privé
Is there an English-speaking instructor?	Y a-t-il un moniteur qui parle anglais?

If the answer's no, then the following will come in handy:

snowplough	chasse-neige
stem christie	stem-christiania
parallel turn	virage parallèle
downhill ski	ski aval
uphill ski	ski amont
Weight on the downhill ski.	Poids sur le ski aval.
Bend your knees.	Pliez les genoux.
Tuck your bottom in.	Redressez-vous.

You're leaning too far back.	Vous vous penchez trop en arrière.
Lean forward.	Penchez-vous en avant.
Traverse the piste ...	Traversez la piste ...
slowly	lentement
faster	plus vite
Slow down.	Ralentissez.
Stop.	Stop.
Follow me.	Suivez-moi.
Shoulders towards the valley.	Rotation des épaules vers l'aval.
Unweight your skis.	Déchargez vos skis.
Transfer your weight now.	Transférez le poids d'un ski sur l'autre.
left/right	gauche/droit
herring bone	montée en ciseaux
side-stepping	montée en escalier
side-slipping	dérapage
Poles behind you.	Les bâtons derrière vous.
Edge/Flatten your skis.	Skis sur les carres/à plat.
Keep your skis parallel.	Gardez vos skis parallèles.
Put your skis together.	Ramenez vos skis.
Keep the skis flat and evenly weighted.	Gardez les skis à plat et répartissez le poids.

Emergencies

I can't move my ...	Je ne peux pas bouger ...
My ... hurts.	... me fait mal.
back	le dos
finger	le doigt
knee	le genou
leg	la jambe
neck	la nuque
wrist	le poignet
I've pulled a muscle.	Je me suis claqué un muscle.
Please get help.	Allez chercher de l'aide, s'il vous plaît.
Don't move.	Ne bougez pas.
avalanche danger	danger d'avalanche
rescue service	équipe de secours

SOME USEFUL EXPRESSIONS (GERMAN)

Equipment

I'd like to hire/buy ...	Ich würde gerne ... mieten/kaufen.
ski boots	Skischuhe
ski poles	Skistöcke
skis	Skier
What length poles/skis should I have?	Wie lang sollten meine Stöcke/Skier sein?
Can you adjust the bindings?	Könnten Sie bitte meine Bindungen einstellen?
Can you wax my skis?	Könnten Sie bitte meine Skier wachsen?
Can you sharpen the edges?	Könnten Sie bitte meine Kanten schärfen?
I am a ...	Ich bin ein ...
beginner	Anfänger
intermediate skier	fortgeschrittener Skiläufer
advanced skier	guter Skiläufer
I weigh ... kilos.	Ich wiege ... Kilo
My shoe size is ...	Meine Schuhgrösse ist ...

British	4	5	6	6½	7	8	8½	9	9½	10	11
Continental	37	38	39	40	41	42	43	43	44	44	45

These boots are ...	Diese Schuhe sind ...
too big/too small	zu gross/zu klein
uncomfortable	unbequem
Do you have any rear-entry boots?	Haben Sie Schuhe mit Hintereinstieg?

Problems

My skis are too long/too short.	Meine Skier sind zu lang/zu kurz.
My ski/pole has broken.	Mein Ski/Stock ist kaputt.
My bindings are too loose/too tight.	Meine Bindungen sind zu locker/zu fest.
The clasp on my boot is broken.	Die Schnalle an meinem Schuh ist kaputt.
My boots hurt me.	Meine Schuhe tun mir weh.

Clothing and accessories

bumbag	Lendentasche
gloves	Handschuhe
goggles	Schneebrille
hat	Mütze
headband	Stirnband
jacket	Jacke
mittens	Fäustlinge
one-piece suit	Overall
polo-neck sweater	Rollkragen-Pullover
rucksack	Rucksack
ski suit	Skianzug
ski trousers	Skihose
socks	Socken
sun glasses	Sonnenbrille

and don't forget:

lip salve	Lippenpomade
sun cream	Sonnencreme

Lifts and lift passes

I'd like a ...	Ich hätte gerne einen ...
lift pass	Skipass
day	Tag
season	Saison
week	Woche
I'd like a book of ... lift coupons.	Ich hätte gerne einen Block mit ... Lift-Coupons.
ten/twenty/thirty	zehn/zwanzig/dreissig
Do I need a photo?	Brauche ich ein Foto?
Could I have a lift-pass holder?	Hätten Sie eine Hülle für den Skipass?
cable car	Luftseilbahn
chair lift	Sessellift
drag lift	Schlepplift
gondola	Gondel
Where's the end of the queue?	Wo ist das Ende der Schlange?
Can I have a piste map, please?	Könnte ich bitte einen Plan der Pisten haben?

On the piste

Where are the nursery slopes?	Wo sind die Anfängerhügel?
Which is the easiest way down?	Welches ist die einfachste Abfahrt
It's a(n) ... run.	Es ist eine ... Abfahrt.
easy/difficult	leichte/schwere
gentle/steep	flache/steile
green (very easy)	grüne (sehr leichte)
blue (easy)	blaue (leichte)
red (intermediate)	rote (mittelschwere)
black (difficult)	schwarze (schwere)
The piste is closed.	Die Piste ist gesperrt.
The piste is very icy.	Die Piste ist sehr eisig.
... snow	... Schnee
deep	Tiefschnee
powder	Pulverschnee
sticky	Pappschnee
mogul (bump)	Buckel
rock	Stein
tree	Baum
Watch out!	Achtung!/Vorsicht!

Ski school

I'd like some skiing lessons.	Ich hätte gerne Skistunden.
group/private	Gruppe/privat
Is there an English-speaking instructor?	Gibt es einen englisch-sprachigen Lehrer?

If the answer is no, then the following will come in handy:

snowplough	Schneepflug
stem christie	Stemm-Christiania
parallel turn	Parallelschwung
downhill ski	Talski
uphill ski	Bergski
Weight on the downhill ski.	Talski belasten.
Bend your knees.	In die Knie.
Tuck your bottom in.	Hüften nach vorne.
Lean forward.	In die Vorlage.
Traverse the piste ...	Die Piste ... überqueren.

slowly	langsam
faster	schneller
Slow down.	Bremsen.
Stop.	Stop.
Follow me.	Folgen Sie mir.
Shoulders towards the valley.	Schultern talwärts.
Up-down-up.	Hoch-tief-hoch.
Unweight your skis.	Skier entlasten.
Transfer your weight now.	Verlagern Sie jetzt Ihr Gewicht.
left/right	links/rechts
herring bone	Grätenschritt
side-stepping	Treppenschritt
side-slipping	seitwärts rutschen
Poles behind you.	Stöcke nach hinten.
Edge/Flatten your skis.	Kanten belasten/Skier laufen lassen.
Keep your skis parallel.	Halten Sie Ihre Skier parallel.
Put your skis together.	Halten Sie die Skier zusammen.
Keep the skis flat and evenly weighted.	Skier laufen lassen und beide gleich belasten.

Emergencies

I can't move my ...	Ich kann mein(en) ... nicht bewegen.
My ... hurts.	Mein ... tut weh.
back	Rücken
finger	Finger
knee	Knie
neck	Hals
wrist	Handgelenk
I've pulled a muscle.	Ich habe einen Muskel gezerrt.
Please get help.	Bitte holen Sie Hilfe.
Don't move.	Bewegen Sie sich nicht.
avalanche danger	Lawinengefahr
rescue service	Rettungsdienst

INDEX

An asterisk(*) next to a page number indicates a map reference. Where there is more than one set of page references, the one in bold type refers to the main entry. For index to Practical Information, see p. 169.

Adelboden 8*, 20–21, **22–25**, 23*, 100, 102
Andermatt 7*, 20–21, **26–29**, 28–29*, 71
Anzère 8*, 20–21, **30–33**, 31*
Arosa 7*, 20–21, **33–38**, 34–35*, 108
Champéry 8*, 20–21, **39–43**, 40–41*, 44*, 47, 116
Champoussin 8*, 20–21, 40–41*, 44*, **46–48**, 116
Château d'Œx 8*, 20–21, **49–51**, 90*, 127, 128
Crans-Montana 8*, 13, 20–21, 31, 31*, **52–56**, 53*
Crosets, Les 43, 44*, 47
Davos 7*, 13, 20–21, **57–62**, 58–59*, 96, 98, 99, 105
Diablerets, Les 8*, 20–21, 51, **63–67**, 64–65*, 151, 154
Disentis 7*, 20–21, **68–71**, 69*
Engelberg 7*, 20–21, **72–75**, 74–75*
Flims/Laax 7*, 20–21, 71, **76–81**, 78–79*
Grächen 8*, 20–21, **82–84**, 131*
Grindelwald 8*, 20–21, **85–89**, 156, 158–159*, 160
Gstaad 8*, 16, 20–21, 51, **89–92**, 90–91*, 127, 128, 129
Gstaad Superski Region 50, 90, 127, 128
Haute-Nendaz 8*, **93–95**, 141, 142–143*, 146, 148, 149
Jungfrau Region 85, 86, 120, 156, 158

Klosters 7*, 13, 20–21, 57, 59, 60, **96–99**, 97*, 105
Laax, see Flims/Laax
Lenk 8*, 20–21, 22, 25, **100–103**, 101*
Lenzerheide-Valbella 7*, 20–21, **104–109**, 106–107*
Leysin 8*, 20–21, **110–114**, 112–113*
Montana, see Crans-Montana
Morgins 8*, 20–21, 44*, 47, 48, **115–117**
Mürren 7*, 12, 20–21, 86, **118–123**, 158–159*
Pontresina 7*, 20–21, **122–126**, 123*
Portes du Soleil 39, 42, 44–45*, 46, 47, 48, 116, 187
Rougemont 8*, 20–21, 51, 90*, 91, **127–129**
Saas-Fee 8*, 12, 13, 20–21, 27, 83, 84, **130–134**, 131*, 186
St. Moritz 7*, 16, 20–21, 90, 105, 124, 126, **135–140**, 136–137*
Valbella, see Lenzerheide-Valbella
Verbier 8*, 13, 16, 20–21, 93, 94, **141–147**, 142–143*, 148, 149
Veysonnaz 8*, 20–21, 93, 141, 142*, **148–150**
Villars 8*, 20–21, 51, 63, 66, **151–155**, 152–153*
Wengen 8*, 12, 13, 20–21, 85, 86, 120, **156–161**, 158–159*
Zermatt 8*, 10, 12, 13, 16, 20–21, 27, 83, 84, 126, 132, 140, **162–168**, 163*, 186